Flipping Houses

The Millennials guide to quitting your job and learning the secrets the real estate industry don't want you to know about

AJ SMITH

© **Copyright 2019 - All rights reserved.**

The content contained within this book may not be reproduced, duplicated or transmitted without direct written permission from the author or the publisher.

Under no circumstances will any blame or legal responsibility be held against the publisher, or author, for any damages, reparation, or monetary loss due to the information contained within this book. Either directly or indirectly.

Legal Notice:

This book is copyright protected. This book is only for personal use. You cannot amend, distribute, sell, use, quote or paraphrase any part, or the content within this book, without the consent of the author or publisher.

Disclaimer Notice:

Please note the information contained within this document is for educational and entertainment purposes only. All effort has been executed to present accurate, up to date, and reliable, complete information. No warranties of any kind are declared or implied. Readers acknowledge that the author is not engaging in the rendering of legal, financial, medical or professional advice. The content within this book has been derived from various sources. Please consult a licensed professional before attempting any techniques outlined in this book.

By reading this document, the reader agrees that under no circumstances is the author responsible for any losses, direct or indirect, which are incurred as a result of the use of information contained within this document, including, but not limited to, — errors, omissions, or inaccuracies.

Table of Contents

INTRODUCTION   9

CHAPTER 1: PREPARING FOR CHANGE AS A 9-5 MILLENNIAL   11

The Lie of the 9-5   13

Mindset Madness   17

Habit vs. Mindset   19

Are You Ready To Move Forward?   21

Investing In Yourself by Investing In House Flipping   22

CHAPTER 2: BACK TO BASICS   25

House Flipping – What is it?   25

How Does The Process Work?   26

Assumptions of House Flipping   27

More Secure Than A Safe?   31

Risky Business   33

Dream Goals   36

Why You Should Do It Anyway   39

Would It Be Worth It?   40

CHAPTER 3: SECRETS OF THE REAL ESTATE INDUSTRY   43

CHAPTER 4: GETTING TAKEN SERIOUSLY AS A MILLENNIAL   49

Dealing With Student Loan and General Debt When Investing   51

CHAPTER 5: THE WORK BEGINS   53

Building a Team   53

What Are Your Timescales?   55

The Search Begins   57

CHAPTER 6: FINDING PROPERTY TO FLIP   67

Apartments and Condominiums   67

Pros   67

Foreclosures   70

External Factors   73

CHAPTER 7: COVERING YOUR BASES   79

The Laws Associated With and Essential Due Diligence Needed For Flipping Properties   79

The Checklist   84

Don't Get Rose Tinted Glasses   88

CHAPTER 8: FINANCING   91

How Much Cash Do You Require To Start A Flip?   91

Picking the Best Option   96

Formula Needed To See If a Property Will Be Popular   97

CHAPTER 9: FORMULAS YOU NEED TO KEEP IN LINE   99

CHAPTER 10: RENOVATING   102

DIY vs. Contracting   105

Quick Fixes   110

Outside Revamp   113

CHAPTER 11: SELL THAT HOUSE   117

Increasing the Value of the Property   117

Attracting Buyers   121

Negotiate and Close   123

CLOSING THE DEAL   125

When No One Is Buying   128

Keeping the Property for Rent   131

CHAPTER 12: THE DO'S AND DON'TS   135

When Things Go Wrong   135

Ongoing Mindset   137

Common Mistakes   139

The Do's And Don'ts of Flipping Houses   139

CHAPTER 13: FINAL CHECKLIST   143

The House Flipping Checklist   143

CHAPTER 14: CONCLUSION   148

BIBLIOGRAPHY

Introduction

Perhaps you have seen many shows on flipping houses, or you know someone who is into it and earns an insane amount of cash from a few transactions every year. Or maybe you are just tired of the vicious cycle of 9-5 and want to retire early and get in on the action. However, you are at a loss as to where to begin and how to go about it.

The truth is; many others have been in your shoes. The sad news is that many them failed even before they succeeded, while some were able to succeed where the others couldn't. What did they do differently? How can you be one of the successful ones?

The great news is you are already taking a significant first step by purchasing this book. In this book, you will be learning everything you need to know concerning the house flipping business. You will equally learn how to locate an ideal home to flip as well as getting the financing you will require for flipping.

This book will lead you through the process of determining if you have the appropriate resources and mindset to purchase, rehab, and sell homes. It will also show you how you can project revenue even before making your initial offer on a property. We will explore these topics and many more.

This book is categorized into various sections to help in achieving your house flipping goals. These include:

- **Section 1 - Mindset**
- **Section 2 - Increasing your knowledge**

- **Section 3 - Finding the right house**
- **Section 4 - Viewing and buying**
- **Section 5 - Making some money**
- **Section 6 - Making the sale**

I do not promise that you won't run into hitches along the line. Being a successful house flipper comes with its own set of problems. But I am confident that when you finish reading this book, you will have an in-depth knowledge of all that it entails to be a successful house flipper. Additionally, if you utilize all of the data this book offers, you will be able to kick-off a successful side business from scratch and seamlessly make revenue.

It has been fun researching for this book. I sincerely hope you will find it easy to grasp while reading.

Now, let us begin the journey to a successful house-flipping business together.

Chapter 1: Preparing for Change as a 9-5 Millennial

Millennials, equally referred to as the Net Generation or Generation Y, consist of a demographic which comes after Generation X. Millennials is a term which is typically used to describe individuals born between 1980 – 2000.

Millennials were raised in a world filled with electronics and connected socially. This generation has attained the most attention from marketing. Because they are the most diverse generation in terms of ethnicity, they are more accepting of differences.

This set of individuals are usually more confident because they were told they were unique. Millennials also have more optimism about America's future in comparison to other generations. This remains the case even though they are the first generation that is expected to attain less economic success in comparison to their parents.

One major result of the optimism many Millennials have is heading into adulthood with unrealistic expectations. Sometimes, this may result in disappointment. Many early Millennials went past post-secondary education only to end up underemployed, in unrelated sectors, or moving between various jobs more regularly than the past generations. Some of them even remain stuck in these dead-end jobs, making other individuals rich instead of engaging in something beneficial to them.

Their expectations may have come from the very involved and

encouraging group of parents we call the helicopter parents today.

Presently, the generation of millennials is dealing with issues in the market as opposed to previous generations. Many millennials are battling to survive in the market. With numerous problems ranging from inflation in the education sector, A.I job screening, less earning than past generations, fast growth in technology, dealing with more college debts, and a host of other issues, the millennials don't find it easy as many of these make it even more complicated for them.

However, technology has given Millennials an edge. Many millennials were raised with the internet and computers with a GUI or graphical user interface. Because they are familiar with all of these, they have a less stressful time understanding visual languages and interfaces. They can adjust quickly to new OS or operating systems, devices, and programs. They are equally more capable of performing tasks that are computer-based faster than in past generations. Although there is proof that multitasking is not an efficient manner of working, Millennials could be the employees that can make it work.

Generally, Millennials don't have issues with the concept of public internet life. From the perspective of the Millennial, privacy is mostly an issue of functional setting that limits who can see what they share online. The level of comfort they have with social media implies that they are great at promoting themselves and great at creating connections via social media.

However, this approach often leads to a problem when they compare themselves with their peers. When it has to do with getting things done, Millennials depend on the internet a lot. If any issue arises with their devices or gadgets, they often head to the internet to look for help in pointing out and correcting these problems.

All of these ensures that this generation has a more in-depth understanding of hardware issues and programming all of which gives them an edge in the current market. One of the edges millennials have with their knowledge of the internet and getting things done is that, they can engage in various kinds of businesses right from the comfort of their homes. This is possible without the need to go into the continuous cycle of the 9-5. A perfect example of this is the business of flipping houses. With their knowledge of technology and the way the internet works, they can be one of the leaders in the business in no time.

The Lie of the 9-5

Speaking frankly, the standard 9-5 job to help someone achieve his/her goals is not fun. You spend all your time working for another individual with minimal freedom. As if that is not enough, the cash you make is not proportional to the amount of work you are putting in.

The great news is that, there are other things you can do which would help you earn all the cash you need without having to compromise your freedom and well-being. One of these is the business of flipping houses. If you go into the business of flipping, you can be your own boss, work during your free time and still remain fulfilled in the process.

But knowing this, why then are a lot of individuals okay with working the 9-5? Let us check out the common misconceptions that encourage this:

Sense of Security

For many individuals, working 9-5 offers them a sense of security knowing they would always get an income within a specific period of the month. This results in people becoming comfortable waiting for that period of the month when their salary comes in.

However, this can't be further from the truth. In a 9-5 job, you only have a false sense of security because your stay the next day is not absolute. It only takes a minor issue to make you lose your job and be left with nothing. If you are told your services are no longer required, you have no other option than to leave, losing that sense of security you cherish.

Set Work Hours

For many people, knowing the set period they would work is refreshing. They understand that after the set 9-5, they are free to do whatever they want and thrive on this. They just work all day and head out when the clock hits 5 pm.

Again, this is another false belief. In many organizations, work goes past the set 5 pm. Numerous times, you even go home with some paperwork depending on your profession. Additionally, the set work period makes it a bit rigid. For instance, if your child needs you during work hours or an emergency arises, depending on your kind of job, you may not be able to leave.

Capacity to Plan Properly

Because of the set 9-5, many people believe they can make

proper plans. They know when they would be busy at work and make plans after work hours.

It's not easy to plan all your activities after 5 pm which is the typical closing time. You may end up missing out on a range of family events which typically take place earlier, and it could be strenuous on both you and your family.

Those are just a few misconceptions people have which makes them remain in 9-5 jobs. However, these jobs are harming you in more ways than you know.

Below are some issues you may deal with if you stay in a 9-5 job.

You Don't Feel Fulfilled

This is very common for most people. Many people are stuck in jobs they never wanted in the first place, either as a means to earn a living or because their parents decided their paths.

You now have the job you desired, and you have a lot of cash. But are you fulfilled? You need to be in a job that you are passionate about and excites you.

Many 9-5 jobs are repetitive and so draining because you wake, rush off to work, head back home and repeat the process once more. It can be a very unfulfilling way to live.

You Are Wasting Valuable Time

Right now, you are likely within the ages of 18 to 60. Your frustrating alarm wakes you up every day. You hit the snooze button numerous times hoping you could just relax today. You know it is impossible and finally, you get up and head to work.

You drag yourself to work where you get to your desk. You will remain here for the next 8 hours. Time seems to be slow, but eventually, it hits 5pm, and you get to go home. Then you realize you have to repeat this process tomorrow and yes, you do the same thing again, until you are in your 60s and almost depressed. For many people, this is not the case, but for a lot of people, this is how it usually goes.

However, you need to note that this time you spent is something you can never get back. It is gone forever. You could have used it in achieving something for yourself instead of someone else.

That is not all. Many individuals are starting to put in more work hours as a result of more bills to be paid among a host of other reasons. You find out that the time you have to yourself is dwindling even more.

Working longer does not mean you would get rich overnight. Instead, it is a terrible idea especially if you plan on achieving any goal for yourself. If you want to achieve your goals and make something of yourself, you need to let go of the 9-5 mindset.

How Can You Do This?
You need to take a step today. There are many things you can try out that would be more fulfilling than taking a 9-5 job.

Don't get me wrong; there is no perfect job out there. You still face a lot of issues if you decide to do your own thing. It comes with a higher reward, but the risks are also high. You won't get any bonuses, raises, or benefits each year. You won't get a paycheck during a stipulated period. However, the potential advantages are way more than the negatives. You need to make that bold move today, and you would have no regrets in the end.

Mindset Madness

A good number of us remain stuck in our present life situation as a result of fear. This is something that comes for a reason. As a species, we have been able to survive with the help of fear. However, that tool that has helped us survive may also be what is keeping you stuck in an unpleasant life situation.

Many of us do not move forward due to many reasons beyond the fear of failure. When we come across the possibility to fail, many of us decide to remain safe and stay where we are as opposed to exposing ourselves to the possibility of failure.

If you want to move forward and get out of your present life situation, you must identify those fears which are preventing you from taking action. Once you do this, you can then deal with them.

Below are some of the characteristics that you would require if you want to achieve this. They are:

Positive Mindset

Your mindset is a collection of beliefs and thoughts that aid in shaping the way you think. Your thought habits have an impact on what you feel, what you do, and the way you think. Your mindset also has an impact on how you see yourself and how you see the world. Your mindset is a huge deal, and if you plan of getting out of your present life situation, it is the first thing you need to work on.

What you channel your mind to is the location you will automatically channel your action to. You need to try to stay positive and believe in yourself the best way you can. A few of the top ways of doing this is to surround yourself with inspiring and positive individuals, write down the progress you have made, and start listening to motivational and positive materials.

Cultivate Grit

You need to be passionate about anything you plan on doing. In this situation, it is the goal you want to achieve, to leave your present life situation. This will ensure the persistence to see it to the end.

Having an in-depth interest in what you want to do is one of the crucial things that will help you stay motivated. If you want to accomplish your goals of leaving your present situation, you need to have the determination to ensure you stay on the right path.

Patience

Patience is not the same as waiting. Waiting does not involve action. By practicing patience, you continue working toward your goals even when the results are not visible yet. If you are waiting without doing any work, you have stopped. Patience means believing in your goal enough to ensure it keeps you moving forward.

Accountability

You need to be responsible for your inner and external life which include your actions, feelings, and thoughts. This is an essential trait to develop. It means you take responsibility for the results of your actions. If you can admit your errors and face the facts while knowing it does not reduce your worth, then you are on the right path to learning accountability.

Self-Confidence

To get past your comfort zone and move further in life, self-confidence is a crucial trait you need. It has to do with your willingness to explore new areas, leave your present situation, take risks, and dive into new things.

The significant part of self-confidence is that you can fake it till you make it. You may have many doubts and fears before you do something, but you will still be able to project confidence, even if you don't have it yet. One of the best ways of developing confidence is to believe that you have what it requires to deal with any uncertainty that may come your way when you take that step forward.

Habit vs. Mindset

Have you ever imagined why it sometimes feels like a battle to get ahead? The reality is that if you want to be successful at what you do, you need to have a high level of discipline in your mindset. The reason is simple; your mindset has a way of affecting your habits.

If, in your mind, you believe that you cannot change a bad habit, then you will never make any effort to correct it. You will stay away from situations that you believe are uncomfortable and may not get anywhere close to your goal.

So what are the habits you need to pick up if you want to achieve success in whatever you are doing and how do you correct your mindset into changing them?

Let's take a look at some ways to do this below:

Let Go of the Fixed Mindset

Individuals who have a fixed mindset believe that talents and habits are traits you cannot change. They also believe that to be successful, all you need is to be talented without making any effort. This is not true.

Successful individuals are aware of this. They channel a lot of time every day in developing a growth mindset, changing how they see things, and learning new skills to improve their lives.

Don't forget that the person you are now, does not have to be who you are tomorrow.

Acknowledge Your Flaws

Perhaps you procrastinate a lot and end up doing things in a rush at the last minute. You can tailor your plans around that. Make reasonable goals and give yourself adequate time to achieve them.

Understand Your Style of Learning

If you can point out the easiest ways for you to learn, you can effectively use your time when trying to achieve a goal. This will let you work using various patterns that work for you, making you achieve goals faster.

Don't Forget That Learning Requires Time

Anything worth doing takes time. You need to be realistic regarding the time it will require for you to achieve the goal you want. You need to move a little step forward each day, but eventually, you are guaranteed to get to your destination.

Are You Ready To Move Forward?

If you want to develop great habits, you need to be ready to change your mindset about the things you can do and the habits you already have. You cannot obstruct your progress with the notion that there is no room for you to change those habits that are not of benefit to you.

You need to take the needed actions to learn, remain motivated and take little steps every day for you to be successful. By determining what works for you and dropping habits that are drawing you back, you will be able to learn great lessons and achieve success in all aspects of your life.

Investing In Yourself by Investing In House Flipping

Most times, when you hear about investment, it is usually about investing money. However, most of these fail to mention that you can equally invest in yourself. Doing this will ensure you make returns that would last through your entire life.

Do you know that you can invest in yourself by investing in house flipping? The possibilities are limitless. The question is, how exactly do you achieve this? That is what we will be covering in this section.

Invest In Your Mind

By investing in your mind, it means you need to read and obtain information concerning house flipping and things that you need to know before investing. You need to understand the basics and find out the core information. All of these will ensure you are ready before you invest.

You Can Earn Continuous Income from Rent Before You Sell

When you invest in a house flipping business, even if you are unable to sell a property, you will be able to earn continuous income via this business. You can re-channel some of the income into the upgrade and maintenance of your property. All of these are expenses which would amount to nothing when you consider the revenue you can get from real estate.

Eventually, when you sell the property, it would have probably risen in value, which would bring you additional revenue.

You Are Protected From the Volatile Market

When you begin a house flipping business, you don't have to deal with the market volatility that Wall Street faces. In the stock market, a bear market can quickly clear out a massive chunk of your financial portfolio. However, in the business of house flipping, these forces are not applicable. By going into a house flipping business, you are going into a secure and stable real estate investment that is going to increase in value with time.

The instant you begin a house flipping business, you join a group of individuals who live conveniently off a reliable and stable investment. To attain success, the important thing is to know that you are investing in a steady income source which you would benefit from down the road. By investing in the house flipping business, you automatically invest in yourself which would be way more beneficial in the long run.

Chapter 2: Back to Basics

House flipping is now a very recognized strategy for investment in the market. In the year 2017, over 200,000 houses were sold through flipping in the US, which was the highest figure for more than a decade before that period.

Numerous Television shows like *Flip or Flop* and *Fixer Upper* have equally aided in enhancing the charm of flipping homes. These shows flaunt the fabulous makeovers alongside profits individuals can get from fixing and flipping.

This is not all. Flipping houses can provide fantastic returns which are around 49.2 percent average ROI. In comparison to other methods of investment, flipping houses is a more practical strategy. You may have to get involved by putting your design skills, creative talent, and knowledge of DIY to the test.

However, before you rush off to purchase a home to flip, it is essential that you at least know the basics of the process. That being said, let us dive in and take a look at the most crucial areas of flipping.

But first, what is house flipping? Let's take a look below.

House Flipping – What is it?

House flipping is when a person who invests in properties decides to purchase a home with the plan of fixing it up and reselling it fast. They will purchase the home and increase its value by carrying out the required repairs, and enhancing the style, design, and systems of the property, before selling the home in a few months for a profit.

House flipping can also be about the purchase and resale of homes or real estate in a market where valuations of homes are on the increase. Here, an investor may locate a great deal or foreclosure, buy the home, and hold on for some months until the value of the home goes up. Then they list the property again for an increased price. This is not the same as the fix and flip method of house flipping, where investors upgrade and repair the homes before they place it on the market.

How Does The Process Work?

To properly flip a house, it involves a considerable amount of work. To properly do this, it is ideal to go with the process: Locate, Finance, Fix, Flip

Let us take a look at each step below:

- **Locate**: determine the houses that will make great deals. You are in search of individuals who just need to sell their properties or motivated sellers. People sell their homes for many reasons. For some, the house is an issue, or the sale of the home can aid them in solving an issue they are facing. Your goal should be to locate these individuals and aid them in solving their issues. However, you need to have a budget in place, and you need to have a peak price you can spend on the purchase of a house.

- **Finance**: House flipping is not like attaining a car loan or mortgage. As opposed to the standard bank loan, you will be in search of lenders who will loan you funds depending on property value. You should only invest your cash if you are capable of doing so.

- **Fix**: This is the aspect that separates those who fail and those who succeed. Fixing a home needs you to monitor contractors to get the job done correctly, track repair costs, and remain within the set budget and timescales to create homes that individuals will want to purchase. It also implies that you should understand how to negotiate with and pay contractors, so they carry out the job properly.

- **Flip**: If you do the steps above the right way, you will have a finished home available at a fair price. This is when you promote the home and learn a host of ways to sell a home to ensure you get returns on your investment.

In summary, the first step is locating a house for sale offering a great deal. Then you provide financing for the deal. Next, you put together a team of contractors and fix the property. The instant you finish the work under budget and on time, you sell for a higher price.

Assumptions of House Flipping

House flipping alongside investment in real estate in general, has the potential to bring in a considerable profit. All through history, owning real estate or dealing in it has been a way to enhance wealth and has become associated with profit.

But now, there are many misconceptions about the business flooding the internet. These myths often stem from pessimism among other reasons. Many of these misconceptions fail to make potential investors understand that there is no perfect deal.

Many these myths are further spread by the public or media and don't even come from those who invest in real estate. To be able to ensure you make a profit and grow, you need to learn these misconceptions and overcome them.

Below, we will be taking a look at some of the most common myths about flipping houses.

You, Will, Get Rich Fast

Many experts on the internet will keep ringing in all their platforms that you will be able to attain wealth with ease. All of which is possible by learning some tricks and purchasing their book.

However, there is no real method of getting rich fast. Similar to other sectors, if you plan on making money or getting rich, you need determination, time, and hard work.

You won't become extremely wealthy from flipping one house. No, you will have to increase your earnings slowly by reducing your risk, taking time, and not looking for shortcuts.

So if you had plans to go on a vacation with a vault full of money after flipping your first home, you might want to have a rethink.

Real Estate Is Very Easy

Learning any form of real estate investment, irrespective of the type, is not easy. It takes a considerable amount of hard work and capital. In the standard house flipping style of renovation and selling, you will require cash to purchase the home, make renovations, and then get back all that you spent along with some extra for it to be beneficial.

All of this means house flipping is not easy, has some risks, and may not be suitable for all individuals.

There Is ALWAYS Risk in Real Estate

Yes, there are sometimes risks that come with real estate. But, you can prevent these risks or at least reduce them drastically. One of the methods of doing this is by wholesaling. A typical fix and flip can be very crucial and risky especially if you are a newbie.

However, a safer option for starters is wholesaling. It can be a great way to start because if you do it correctly, you don't need to expend any of your cash or even borrow. No, to do this, you will locate a property and place it under contract. Next, you locate a buyer. When you close the deal, you get a wholesaler's fee.

Irrespective of the option you decide to go with, you need to ensure you research all it entails.

There Is a Perfect Home You Can Flip

Factors like a great neighborhood, a good foundation, and minimal competition and many more are things you should watch out for when searching for a home to buy.

But, locating all of these on one specific property is almost impossible. Sometimes you may check the other boxes, but the neighborhood is not great. Or you find a great home, but the competition is insane.

There is no perfect home, and there are always going to be obstacles to overcome. Don't spend years searching for the appropriate property to flip. A better option is to pick a home and make your calculations. If it is profitable, then buy it.

To Flip Homes, You Need To Be a Contractor

Yes, having a bit of experience in renovating homes can save you cost. But it is not a necessity to flip houses. Many individuals will instead get a team of contractors in place to aid in the specialized parts. Although this may cost more cash, it is faster than and not as tedious as doing it by yourself.

You Need Loads Of Cash

This is a widespread misconception about this business. Many people believe this business is only for wealthy individuals. Many individuals believe that you need to have loads of income if you plan on buying a property. Yes, cash simplifies things, but you can still purchase a property if you have no personal cash.

So how do you do this? The answer is loans. Many flippers buy properties with the help of loans. If all goes well, you will then be able to get adequate income to begin paying for properties without loans.

More Secure Than A Safe?

Flipping houses comes with a range of positive aspects which range from financial security, long term profit, among a host of others. That is not all. In comparison to a host of investments available, the real estate market can be a more secure choice.

Now let us take a more elaborate look at these, starting from the benefits.

Benefits of Flipping Houses

- **Possibility to Make Great Profit**: This is an undeniable reason to flip houses. For those involved in it full-time, it can be a very profitable venture. You can also make your profit relatively fast in the appropriate circumstances.

- **Report to No-one**: Many individuals involved in the business of house flipping are self-employed, and they don't report to anyone. You will be able to determine your work hours, work from any location, and do anything you love.

- **It is Rewarding to Renovate Homes**: Even if your interest lies in making cash alone, you will find out that the rewards are enormous. When you flip a home, you are providing it with a new life. By renovating, you could be improving the street on which the home is situated. This can be a fulfilling experience.

- **It Encourages Personal Growth:** Purchasing home and materials frequently will aid you in developing your negotiation skills. You will also learn to manage your time, hold others accountable, and delegate tasks. You can channel all of these to various forms of businesses later on.

Why Can The Property Market Be Safer Than Other Investments?

Now, there are a host of options for investments. You can purchase stock, sell bitcoins, or run an online business. However, before you invest your cash, you need to ask yourself a very crucial question:

Which of these is the most secure option?
Real estate has always remained the answer to this. Let us take a look at the reasons why:

- **Inflation**: Properties offer investors security. The value of properties will almost always rise. Irrespective of the kind of property you purchase, during the periods of inflation, the prices will go up. During this period, you get more rewards in comparison to other forms of business.

- **Physiological Satisfaction**: Properties are assets you can see. These will offer investors satisfaction. They get the feeling that they own something as opposed to many other investment options. If you run an online business, and you fail to make sales for a long time, eventually you will be unable to sustain the business.

- However, this is not the case in real estate. If you are unable to sell a home after a while, you can either lease it out or use it.

- **Volatility:** With properties, you are privy to continuous returns for a very long period. As stated by the (NCREIF) or National Council of Real Estate Investment Fiduciaries, commercial properties offered close to 8.4 percent returns in 2000-2010. The reason is that unlike most businesses' which are liable to change, real estate is an industry which is stable and has minimal risks.

- **Rental:** Property investors will be able to invest from a rental income which they get monthly. What is more, it is more stable in comparison to other options of investment. Investors only have to do their findings and locate a great property, rent it to people, and earn cash even when there is a financial downturn. Investors will have more benefits if the property is highly demanded as the income they gain from rental attains more stability. Even if the property market does not grow anymore, it is safe to state that after ten years or more, your property will have more value.

- **Finally, real estate gives anyone the capacity to be an investor.** It is not essential for you to be a professional before you can be a part of it. The instant you know how secure and valuable it can be for you, all you require is the appropriate team to lead you through the entire process.

Risky Business

As opposed to those who build a home, and can control the process from the start to a reasonable extent, 'house flippers' are not always aware of the issues that are lying underneath a building or in those walls.

What this implies is that there are risks to flipping houses. However, there are also ways to mitigate these risks. Below are a few of the main risk factors and solutions in real estate.

Continuously Changing Market

The housing market determines the amount of profit you make from flipping a house. The issue is, this is not always predictable in most situations. Is it presently booming upon buying? Should you hold on for when it drops before you purchase the property? What if it goes up and you never see this great deal anymore? These are questions that keep ringing in the heads of house flippers, and this is for a good reason.

How do you fix this?
Search for market updates from your local real estate agent. Also, you will want to understand the yearly developments in your location to enable you to determine the period the market will be at its lowest and peak.

Demographic Shift

Is there development in the area you are buying? Is it declining or is it stable? Learning how popular a particular area is will help you understand the level of aggression you should utilize when pricing. If you do this the wrong way, you could lose a considerable amount of cash that you could have channeled to other areas.

How do you fix this?
You can find a host of resources online which will readily offer

you this information. Go through real estate websites to find out if new buildings are springing up there or if there is a trend of individuals selling their property in the location.

Inappropriate Tools for the Job

When you initially begin, you may want to get things done on your own. This is to enable you to have an understanding of how things work, so when you begin to hire others to aid with the renovation, you will be aware of what the job entails allowing you to gauge their work better.

There is a core issue if you are beginning from scratch. There is a high possibility that you would not have adequate equipment for the job. This will show on your time and costs.

How do you fix this?
It is crucial that you locate the top equipment without spending too much funds and time. There are great online stores that can help you out with this so long as you know what you are searching for.

No Experience

House flipping, depending on the background you have, can be a very frightening venture. This is the case especially if you don't have as much experience as others do when they are getting into the field. Aside from this, flipping houses is a gamble and one which can be very costly. That is why you don't want to take a wrong step due to inexperience.

How do you fix this?
Aside from gaining more experience, it will be beneficial to

reach out to someone you know who is into the business to aid you in your initial project. This will enable you to have a little understanding of what house flipping involves.

Hidden or Unknown Repairs

Every house comes with them, perhaps even the one you live in presently. You will discover most of these during the renovation, irrespective of if this implies breaking down a wall or creating a more open room and other hidden issues you were not aware of initially.

How do you fix this?
This is inevitable. However, you could include it in the budget you have for repairs. Ensure you stick to your budget and have around 20 percent extra in the event you are not estimating the price accurately. The great thing about this is if you don't spend the cash, you will pocket more profit.

Flipping houses comes with its risks, and it is not for the fainthearted. You will have some sleepless and restless nights and possibly down times, but it works out eventually.

If you can avoid or adequately manage the risks involved in flipping, you will be able to get the benefits offered by this profitable venture.

Dream Goals

A house flipping business can be very profitable. However, it is only possible if you do it smartly. Irrespective of your objective, there are some strategies you need to follow when setting up your goals.

Every person in the business of house flipping should have a vision board containing the goals they plan to achieve from flipping houses. All of your objectives must also be SMART.

Let us take a look at how to make this possible below:

First SMART stands for Specific, Measurable, Achievable, Realistic, and Time-Bound.

Specific

Having decided that you want to be in the business of flipping homes, you need to ensure your goal is specific. It is not ideal for you to just say; *"I want to be successful in flipping homes"* without dipping your hands into the fundamental aspects which consist of creating a specific goal.

Here, you need to raise numerous questions ranging from:

- Do I plan on investing in a single strategy and have continuous income?

- Am I planning on going full-time or part-time?

- Do I want to use the fix and flip technique?

- Do I want a short term or long term investment?

Creating goals would aid you in choosing the best way to invest because you have made them specific. If you don't have a specific goal, it may be difficult to achieve your goals because you won't have a focus.

Measurable

You must be able to measure all of your house flipping goals. You can't just say you want to be among the top house flippers or the best flipper in this region. No. Instead, a measurable goal could be:

- I want to have a 20% return on any investment I make
- I want a monthly income of $3000 from my investment

When you have a measurable goal, it can aid you in assessing your house flipping goals with ease.

Achievable

When going into the business of house flipping, ambition and passion are great. They are traits that will aid you in best achieving what you want to achieve. However, you need to know that these alone are not adequate.

Your goals need to always be attainable and achievable, especially if you are just beginning. You need to set goals that you can achieve within a specific period. These goals must be possible using the resources at your disposal.

It is impossible for you to become a millionaire from your first house flip. If you set a goal like this, it may result in frustration. To determine if you can attain a goal or not, you need to do your calculations and ensure you get the appropriate numbers.

Realistic

When you set up a house flipping goal, it has to be realistic. You need to know your resources, funding, and your timescale for a flip. Then, you set goals based on them. For instance, it is not possible to look for great properties to sell on your own when you have a full-time job. You need to ensure your goals are realistic, so you don't give up your dream even before you start.

Time-bound

You need to time all aspects of your investment plan. You can't just say you want to earn $20,000 without including a set time. This is applicable even for long term plans. You could break them into smaller timed plans.

You can take advantage of tools for market analysis to get the history of a specific area alongside its real estate. This will provide you with a better idea on the time you would require to achieve a specific goal there, irrespective of if it is a short or long term goal.

In essence, you need to set your goals and using the SMART criteria will help you channel your attention to areas that would help you make a profitable investment.

Why You Should Do It Anyway

If you belong to the category of individuals who enjoy watching various shows on house flipping, it may be tempting to leave your full-time job and dive right into house flipping.

After all, you are certainly going to make a lot of cash fast and without any hassle. All of these would be possible so long as you do the proper search, right? WRONG!!

Flipping is a business with its own set of risks. For this reason, you need to approach it seriously. Factually speaking, it does not differ from other kinds of businesses. If done the right way, you can make a lot of profit. However, if you make a mistake or the circumstances are not in your favor, similar to other businesses, you can take huge losses.

The truth is that it has to do with vast amounts of capital which you get mostly from financing. It is also a little challenging to make as much cash as you would want when vital aspects of the business, like land, don't come cheap.

You may enjoy it when the market goes up, but there are always market downturns which pose a serious risk. If you head into the market late and there is a turn, you may end up losing a lot. If you purchased a property and invested 10% of its value doing renovations and there is a 40% drop in the market, you will amass major losses. You may not be able to sell your property as fast as you want and you would have loans to deal with.

If your dream is to leave your full-time job and head into house flipping, you need to understand that there are still risks involved. You should also remember that not every home you flip brings you profit.

Would It Be Worth It?

You may be wondering; would it be worth it in the end? The answer is YES!!

House flipping, irrespective of its risks, still offers a lot of benefits. In the business, you would learn a lot of life long lessons and develop relationships that would be beneficial to you in the long run.

You will also learn how to manage people which is what you would be doing the majority of the time when you have to deal with contractors and other members of your team.

Also, you will become conversant with the real estate market and hone the capacity to spot great properties to invest in. Finally, the possibility to make returns on your investment is huge. Everyone loves making returns on investments right?

If you can acknowledge the risks that come with this business and go into it with a leveled head, armed with all the proper information you would need, in the end, it all would be worth it.

Chapter 3: Secrets of the Real Estate Industry

The real estate market can be difficult for everyone involved, whether you are an investor, buyer, agent or seller. At a moment, the market can be at its peak and another it could go downwards. The only method of becoming an expert in real estate and draw in a reasonable amount of profit is to get tips from the best.

The sad news is that most of the industry experts who understand the workings of the market are not willing to share the information they have with others. However, in this chapter, you will be learning some of the insider secrets real estate agents would not tell you.

They include:

Open Houses Are Not Functional

Open houses no longer have the effect they used to. Previously, when you had plans to sell a home, the only method of letting buyers inspect your property was to invite them into your house by setting up a meeting with the agent who listed your home or through an open house.

However, presently, if your buyer wants to check out your home, they will be able to head online to any of the numerous websites and see what is in your home without taking a step out.

The fact is that open houses do not work. Agents do not host open houses to help you sell homes. They do it to get more clients who want to sell homes. The truth is that in most locations, you have a higher chance of winning the lottery than selling your home via an open house.

Marketing Is Your Major Job

If you plan to sell a home, the major reason for getting the services of a Realtor is marketing. The job of the realtor is to get as many serious buyers to your property so you can sell your home for the highest price. The fundamental part of Real Estate is marketing, and if a Realtor is not aware of how to market, then the commission is not worth paying.

Numerous Realtors stay away from the issue of marketing and instead try to confuse you with various terms.

Every Agent Is Not Equal

Similar to all industries, there are different levels of competence in the world of Real Estate. However, many individuals believe that all agents are similar. It's best to request contracts from all agents you are granting an interview to beforehand, and prepare questions you would need them to answer.

Overestimations in Listings Only Result In Disappointment

Similar to the way people overestimate their ages on websites or add a picture that makes them look more appealing than they are, the result always remains the same, even in real estate. It can help in capturing attention in the short term, but when the physical meeting occurs, these overblown claims result in disappointment.

If your home is situated far from a busy town, don't exaggerate in your listings and claim it is very close. It is best to use what is available in your property to describe its principal features. If you do not do this, it may result in disappointment for buyers.

Large Agencies Are Not Essential

Yes, more prominent agencies may do well in enhancing recognition and working with huge marketing budgets, but they are also not as willing to negotiate when it has to do with commissions. Smaller agencies can offer you enhanced customer service alongside a personal touch. What is more, with the strength of the internet, you don't need to invest so much budget into marketing like before. Any option that works best for you is the one you need to take.

The Contract Has a Fine Print

Your agent might not inform you, but this is something you need to look out for carefully. You want to look out for any waivers of rights and disclaimers critically. Take the time you require and don't let anyone rush you. Great agents are patient.

You also need to remember that even though your agent is representing you, they are also representing themselves and are on the lookout for what benefits them the most professionally. Ensure they are looking out for your interest as well.

You Can Always Negotiate Commissions

The popular industry standard is 6% for commissions which seller agents and buyers share amongst themselves. However, it is not compulsory for you to follow this. There is nothing you can't negotiate.

Home Inspectors May Not Let You In On Everything

Most individuals who want to buy a home, always insist that a licensed home inspector does the examination before the sale. This is not wrong, but there are inspectors all over the internet who have made claims that agents have urged them not to be too comprehensive during the process of inspection.

Many inspectors learn fast that if they plan on being hired, they can't scare buyers by telling them all issues in the home. Also, some shady agents may work alongside inspectors they share a relationship with to ignore major issues and only point out minor ones.

If you are purchasing a home, do your research on your own to locate an inspector that has a high rating you can depend on to point out even little issues that may hamper your decision to make a purchase.

Renting Is More Sensible

Real estate agents would most likely not reveal to you that it is not right for you to buy, but it may cross their minds. In many situations, it is a better choice for you in terms of finance to rent out a property because the cost is lower and it gives you the desired flexibility if you need to relocate fast.

This is not all. You won't have to spend much to carry out repairs when issues come up. See it like this: by renting, if there is an issue with your heating system, you won't be the one spending money for repairs. It would be the duty of some other person.

When you own a home, you are at more risk. If stuff goes wrong, you may end up losing all you have.

There you have it. These are a few of the secrets real estate agents do not want you to know. Use them to your advantage to get a better result.

Chapter 4: Getting Taken Seriously As a Millennial

Similar to all younger generations, millennials often battle with being taken seriously in all areas ranging from work to business. This is valid since they are high-maintenance, lazy, and not willing to do the work right? No, WRONG!

These are a few of the popular stereotypes. Millennials tend to deal with, spread by the media. Many people believe this which makes it even more difficult for others to take them seriously.

With all of these, how do you get taken seriously when negotiating with others as a Millennial? The tips below may be of help.

Work On Your Overall Grammar

Young generations often utilize slangs. This situation has been made worse due to text messaging. However, grammar is still essential. You need to edit every proposal and correspondence carefully. You have to closely pay attention to the language you use when you speak.

Dress Professionally

The generation of Millennials is one that is seen to be more casual in comparison to others. You need to understand this perception and try to dress in a way that suits your business. During a negotiation, if you turn up in crazy jeans, no one would take you as seriously as you want.

Have Great Etiquette

It is essential that you arrive at every meeting on time. Keep to call schedules with buyers or whomever you are negotiating with. Do not make this myth of Millennials being lazy seem accurate. You need to show up prepared to take action.

Speaking of etiquette, always be early for all meetings, calls, and events. You need to dispel the myth that millennials are lazy, so show up ready for action!

Have A Great Pitch

Be ready with an excellent closing pitch during a sale. When you come prepared, it makes you seem more serious and in turn results in you being taken more seriously.

Know Your Limits

You need to be realistic about negotiations. Keep to your final number and don't change it for anyone. This way, if a buyer keeps dragging for too long, and the buyer fails to meet your range, you can turn down the offer. Any serious buyer who sees you are not willing to budge will make the purchase if he/she is interested.

Remain Calm

After you have begun negotiations, you may start to panic like you have gone past your boundaries. This may result in you quickly accepting a counteroffer to let the process ends. If you have a range and you are aware that it is realistic, there is no need to panic. Keeping calm during a negotiation will ensure any serious buyer also takes you seriously.

Be Civil

Making threats during negotiation may seem like a great move, but it is not. If you threaten to leave the negotiation during every counter offer, some buyers would see it as immaturity and would not take you seriously. Counter offers are normal, so irrespective of how unrealistic a counter offer is; you don't need to start dishing out threats due to anger. Always ensure your tone is friendly and civil even when your range is bold.

Dealing With Student Loan and General Debt When Investing

In an ideal world, you can decide to invest and clear off general debts and student loans simultaneously. If you have the income to deal with both objectives at the same time, and still have adequate cash to have a comfortable life, then this is undoubtedly the route you need to take. It will help in balancing your financial situation and would offer you more feeling of control over the entire process.

However, if the income you have is not adequate to deal with both simultaneously, you will have to split them and face one at a time. Pick the most crucial goal to you, which has the likelihood of having the most significant positive impact in less time.

If your student loan debt has a significantly sizeable monthly payment when you compare it to your income, your only logical option may be to focus on clearing off your debts. Until you are through, you just would be unable to attain the cash you need to make significant investments.

However, if the monthly payments are not an issue, and would instead invest and have the idea that it is more important to invest in long-term security, then do it. All you need to do is ensure you are okay with carrying your debts for a significant amount of time.

There is no appropriate path to take here. You need to choose the strategy you think would be ideal for you.

Chapter 5: The Work Begins

Building a Team

When it has to do with flipping homes, having a team of experts with the know-how at your disposal can help in saving you money and time. In this section, we will be taking a look at the critical individuals you should consider including in your team.

Realtor

Realtors are aware of new properties and real estate listings available. You can easily find them by running a precise internet search for them in a specific geographic location.

Realtors can help you carry out a Comparative Market Analysis on properties you have an interest in. They are also crucial in your marketing plan.

CPA

The inclusion of an accountant or CPA in your team is solely dependent on you. If you have a sizeable business in house flipping, you may want to include a CPA in your daily activities.

The CPA will offer you advice on tax requirements and advantages. He/she will also aid you in preparing tax statements and keeping track of your business costs.

Real Estate Lawyer

There is nothing as terrible as a deal going awry because you did not have great legal advice. You might be tempted to do it by yourself, but this can be a huge mistake.

An actual real estate lawyer who has experience in your local market is crucial to your team. Great attorneys ensure you do not get in trouble.

You most certainly can't know all the laws guiding real estate investment so doing it on your own can never end well. Seek the services of an expert who does. A reliable real estate lawyer will aid you in simplifying the range of documents you need for all transactions. They will also ensure you smoothly and quickly go through the entire process.

Contractor

Many house flippers pick the DIY option when it has to do with property renovation. Whether it is a total home remodel or a fast fix, many individuals choose this option.

If you have comprehensive experience in building, then, of course, doing it yourself is the way to go. However, if you are not very experienced, you may be making a huge mistake. If all you need to fix are minor repairs, like cleaning and painting, then a general contractor may not be necessary. But, if you are doing an elaborate renovation, it is essential to get an experienced general contractor.

A general contractor helps in monitoring the progress of your real estate project. He earns a small percentage of the entire work as his payment. They manage the carpenters, electricians, plumbers, and other handymen. They ensure you don't have to deal with the daily renovation activities, leaving you to focus on other crucial parts like marketing.

Insurance Agent

When it comes to investing in real estate, insurance is an expense lot of individuals often overlook. Also, when you operate without a great policy, it may result in you facing a liability alongside damage to your overall reputation. It is essential for a great insurance agent to have complete knowledge regarding the structure of your business and how you need to insure your property based on your business goals and plan. They will equally be able to direct you on the kinds of insurance you require as regards location and other forms of real estate investments.

Insurance differs based on the kind of real estate you are investing in, and an insurance agent will know which is ideal for your investments. Trying to determine this by yourself or failing to get insurance entirely can result in issues later on, which makes adding an experienced insurance agent to your team very essential.

There you have it; these individuals above will help in covering you those areas you are lacking.

What Are Your Timescales?

Your timescale is going to have an impact on the speed at which you can buy a property, the time it would take you to renovate, and how fast you sell it. Your timescale has a direct impact on your budget and the overall strategy you use in flipping houses. It is crucial for you to properly renovate a property you plan on flipping, but you need to ensure you follow your set timescales.

You can complete most flips in 2 weeks or more and sell them in some months. For each day the property remains yours, the carrying costs will be on you, which can cut into your returns. When developing your timeframe, you will want to have an outline of how long you foresee the project lasting and the number of projects you believe you can finish within specific periods.

In reality, the amount of time required to flip a property can vary between projects which is why your timescale can have an impact on the kind of property you purchase. The guide below will give you a realistic idea on the timescale of your investment to aid you in selling your property fast.

Purchasing the Property: 6-10 Days

It is ideal to note that 6-10 days is an optimistic timescale and it may differ if you are buying your property via a standard means. If you buy your property via an auction or realtor, it can drastically increase the timescale. It might require months to locate a good deal. If you want something that saves time, buying from a wholesaler is a great idea.

Renovation of the Property: 40- 90 Days

If you want a fast renovation, you need to have an efficient team ready. With the appropriate resources and links to great workmen, who know how to complete what you want effectively, renovations can be fast.

Sale of the Property: 50 Days – 6 months

Here things may become dicey. The way you choose to sell your property can decide how slow or fast this process would be. If you choose to make a listing on MLS, you will be able to pay for various listing lengths which could be anywhere from 6 months to as much as a year.

For instance, let us assume you advertise for twelve days, after which you are left with some serious offers. Then you can go into an escrow with a buyer who has funding which takes 20-45 days to close based on the funding they have. If all goes well, you could be done with a sale in 80 days.

However, you need to understand that all of these are estimates which should only help with the creation of your timescales.

The Search Begins

Now you understand the market and determined the kind of property you want to invest your funds. Now, the next step is to locate properties that suit your specifications. So how do you go about it?

This chapter will cover all the range of options you have when it comes to sorting this out.

Let us take a look at some of the top options below:

Check Out Auctions

If you are capable of paying cash when purchasing a property, checking out a private auction, sheriff's sale, or estate auction can be a great idea.

Numerous weeks before a sale, a majority of the lists for foreclosure auction are listed by the county. Adverts for private and estate auctions are run weeks before. If you go through these websites, you will have the chance to find a property before the date of the sale.

One thing to note, however, is that, although you will be able to check out the property or home from the street, you won't have the capacity to go closer for in-depth inspection. Doing this could mean trespassing and put you in the risk of legal actions.

Purchasing at an active auction comes with the danger of being too drawn into the bidding. During the start of a bidding war, many bidders don't remember their budget and bid way above what they initially planned. If you are making a bid for property against others, you need to remember your set limit and ensure you do not deviate from it.

While the profit potential is high when you buy at an action, there is equally an additional risk. Many auctioneers will need you to place 10 percent of the price of purchase beforehand when you win a bid. You will also need to make the remainder of the payment after the auction in no more than 30 days. Failure to do this means you forgo your deposit. For this reason, this method of purchase is not for individuals who do not want to take a risk during house flipping.

It can be tough to get financing for auction purchases as well. Majority of the lenders will need an assessment or at minimum a physical inspection of the property before you close the deal. However, this is not usually possible during an auction. What this implies is that you need to be able to pay cash during purchase, then, later on, get financing for the property.

Speak to Wholesalers

Wholesalers deal in locating properties you can renovate, place them on a contract, and then search for a buyer who will carry out the house flip. In essence, the buyer will take the wholesaler's place in the contract, and pay a fee to the wholesaler to be the intermediary.

Although this method of purchasing properties for house flipping is not cost efficient, it can save you money and time in the long run. Many wholesalers do this full time and have great connections in specific environments and to specific sellers and agents.

If you have an interest working alongside a wholesaler, you will be able to locate them via a search online and in investment groups for real estate.

Use Classifieds

The sad news is that using a daily newspaper as a means of selling properties has gone down drastically. Although numerous local newspapers have not stopped running classified ads for available homes in their online and offline versions, it is not seen as the ideal source of locating a property you want to buy.

It can take a lot of time to go through a newspaper. This is because listings cover substantial geographical areas without a means of searching for precise characteristics and locations electronically. In this era, with the advancement of technology, this can feel outdated and almost not possible to achieve.

Numerous websites that list in the MLS section, including Craigslist, has ensured that searching for real estate investment digitally is now a standard in almost all areas of the US. As stated above, internet searching can provide access to listings by owners and brokers of properties.

Find an Agent

Getting an agent can be an efficient method of speeding up your search for a home to flip. Agents will know the top places to flip homes, which will give them the capacity to filter options applicable to you and offer you extra real estate investment tips for your house flip and property purchase.

Getting an agent who has a specialty in REO can equally be an excellent method of locating properties you can flip. This has to do with properties the guarantor or lender holds due to a defaulted loan. The majority of these houses will have experienced an elaborate foreclosure, and probably a process of eviction.

Additionally, the former occupants did not do much to maintain and care for the property during the period of foreclosure, mortgage default, and eviction. Due to this, many properties come at a price less than the homes around it as a result of their desperate situation which makes them great for a house flip.

Many loan services and lenders create a relationship with a

little group of realtors who specialize in the sales of these kinds of properties. To find them for your flip and fix, all you need to do is work alongside a realtor that has information on these listings alongside the recent rehab houses available on the market. You will have the capacity to do this with ease by searching specifically for REO brokers and real estate agents in a particular geographic location on the internet.

Short Sale

When the owner of a home fails to pay his/her mortgage, they may be provided the option of selling the home "short" by the bank. This could also mean selling the property for lower than the amount owed on the mortgage.

Sometimes, banks will pick this option over foreclosure. This is due to the pricey and time-consuming process they must go through if they want to sell foreclosed properties. If the bank approves a home's short sale, this could create a fantastic chance for a buyer to get a property at a reduced price from the owner of a home who would want the property off his/her hands fast.

There are a few drawbacks to purchasing a property on short sale. First, it may take more time to complete the sale in comparison to a standard sale. This is because the short sale, as well as sale price, must get approval from the lender. Additionally, the lender who approves hardly agrees to pay for any additional which a reasonable seller would agree to make. This could imply that the buyer is left with more closing costs.

That being said, similar to any other source, you will be able to locate houses you can flip in short sales, so do not push them aside. Head to a real estate agent and make inquiries concerning short sale listings. Search for terms like pre-foreclosure, subject to bank approval, or pre-approved by bank, as these all portray that the home is on a short sale.

Use REO

If no one buys a home that has been foreclosed during an auction, the lender or bank becomes the owner. These houses are categorized as REO, or Real Estate Owned listings. Because banks do not have a connection with the purchase and sales of homes, the majority of them will be glad to dispose of these properties from their accounts. For this reason, you are most likely going to get it for a great bargain.

Some lenders send out a REO property list via newsletters or emails. However, investors can equally reach out to their local banks and inquire if they are trying to dispose of properties. It is advisable to be wary of major damage to the property and liens before you make a purchase.

Seller direct

When the prices of home are at the peak, and the market is reasonably healthy, it can be tedious to locate homes to flip. You may not find some of the top deals on the market because the seller has not even decided to sell yet. Seller Direct, also referred to as Direct-to-Seller implies reaching out to homeowners at calculated periods. Like before they list their homes and making them an offer on their house which is not on the market yet.

There are tools like Rebogateway and PropStream among a host of others which use the data available to the public like public transfer, utility, and post office, to develop a tendency to sell models. This will aid in predicting when the owner of a home will be more likely to sell. The instant an opportunity is spotted, the providers of this service will allow you to send marketing collateral alongside targeted emails to prospective sellers. You can head to their websites for more information.

The most recognized platform for seller direct is HomeVestors. They are a franchise with a range of recurring and one-time transaction fees. You will be provided access to a broad range of real estate expertise in return, alongside marketing capacities, and an elaborate network which you can utilize in making offers on houses all over the nation.

Take a Drive Around

This is a conventional means of locating the first property you can flip. All you need to do is head into your car and take a drive around the neighborhood you have in mind. Watch out for properties with distress signs like overgrown yards, heaps of newspapers and mails, boarded windows, among a host of other signs.

If you locate a property like this, put down the home address and do some research on the internet to locate the seller or owner. This will enable you to make an offer and who knows? You may be getting the deal of a lifetime.

Find Listings on the Internet

You can find a host of lists on the internet which show short sales and foreclosures, alongside distressed properties. Dependent on the kind of list, they may be categorized by town, zip code, and city. These lists are great places to check when searching for homes to flip.

You can get a host of these list for free, and you need to purchase some. Begin with the free lists as they may contain what you want. Nowadays, it is becoming much easier to locate listings that would make you great returns after flipping.

There are numerous websites available for investors to take advantage of ranging from BankForeclosureSale.com and BankForeclosedListings.com among a host of others.

Join a Group for Real Estate Investment

During the past few years, real estate investment groups have become popular. There is a probability there are a few in your location, and it might be a great idea to check them out. They can offer opportunities for networking and education which can be beneficial during your search for a flappable home. Also, real estate listings also show up on the monthly newsletters and websites of these group.

There are equally a host of online forums that can aid you in purchasing a property. There are numerous websites like Biggerpockets.com that provide you in-depth information on opportunities for real estate. You can also find a host of real estate investment groups on LinkedIn and Facebook. Many of these groups will also provide you with access to meetups. Here, you will have the chance to have a face-to-face meeting with other prospective property sellers and investors.

Being smart when it has to do with investing in properties can be a challenge, and you will have to employ a host of methods to locate the one that works for you. When you try a bit harder when trying to flip a home, the benefits will be worth it. You will make numerous offers that sellers would not accept. But in the long run, if you continue and maintain discipline, you will attain success in locating the appropriate property.

Chapter 6: Finding Property to Flip

Apartments and Condominiums

A condominium which is commonly referred to as condo is a private residence located within a large community, whereas an apartment is a residence which you lease. This can also be located within a large community. Condo owners are mandated to pay monthly dues that will help keep the amenities in the community running, unlike apartments.

How profitable is it to invest in condos? Below, we shall talk about the benefits and drawbacks of investing in condos that would help you take the right decision.

Pros

- **A lower price of purchase.** The low purchase cost of a condo is one of its major benefits. It is most often more affordable than a single-family house located within the same community. Taxes are less, and the dwelling insurance is not as much as that of a single-family house. Areas beyond the walls are insured by the condominium which results in cheaper insurance.

- **More amenities for tenants.** Owners of condos enjoy amenities such as swimming pools and exercise rooms, unlike single-family homeowners. Mowing of lawns and cutting of shrubs is also taken care of, making them more desirable.

- **Fewer maintenance problems.** The association is responsible for a majority of the maintenance that needs to be done on the exteriors, so it's hardly ever a problem for investors.

- **Fewer repairs to make.** Since it is not the responsibility of the condo owner to repair the exteriors, it lessens the cost of repairs. Any renovation or repair that needs to be done, such as landscaping or installing a new roof, is taken care of by the condominium association.

- **Buyer's market.** There is always a market for condos unless the real estate market in your community is hot.

- When considering the pros of anything the cons should not be left out. Now let's examine the cons involved at investing in condos.

- Cons

- **Monthly association dues.** The monthly association dues consume the savings you made from the low purchase cost, insurance, and taxes. It is essential to find out how much the association dues cost before investing in a condo.

- **Government rules can make it more difficult to sell a condo.** Government regulations designed to reduce the risk of mortgage holders makes it difficult for condo owners who desire to sell their property to get suitable buyers. There are also restrictions placed on condo communities having a higher number of rental units than occupied units by USA Federal Housing Administration (FHA) lenders. Communities with many foreclosures are not left out on the restrictions either

- **Condos are not as easy to sell.** It might take a longer time to get a buyer when you eventually decide to sell your property. There has been a drastic drop in the number of condos permitted for FHA mortgage. This makes it more difficult to sell for a reasonable price as mostly cash buyers are readily available and not willing to pay the full asking price.

- **Condos get a price increase last when there is a recovery.** Single-family homes recover faster after a fall than most condos, and there is always a market for single-family houses even though they are more expensive than the condos.

- **During a down market, they are the first to drop.** Between the years 2007 and 2010, there was a housing market collapse. This led to the foreclosure of numerous condominium communities. It resulted in a reduction of the value of condos after first-time buyers of homes lost their jobs. They had no other real source of income were forced to hand over their property to the bank.

- **Unplanned evaluations can dip into your profits.** Unexpected renovations or repair can dig a hole in the pockets of condo associations. This will cause the value of the condo to reduce. Make necessary enquiries before you invest in a condo.

These restrictions pose a challenge which makes it even more challenging to get buyers as well as those who would be willing to pay well for the property.

After evaluation, it is up to the investor to decide if investing in a condo property is worth it.

Foreclosures

One of the most popular methods of buying a house is through a mortgage. The modus operandi is that the potential house owners make periodic down payments until the completion of the payments. A grace period is given upon default of payment, but after a specified period of grace, if homeowners still fail to meet up, the bank will repossess the house.

It is usually heartbreaking when these potential house owners lose their houses because of their inability to pay for it. This, however, serves as one of the best opportunities for you to make money as these homes are usually offered at a reasonable price.

As great as this sounds, it is essential that other factors are put into consideration before buying these houses. The reason is that most of these foreclosed houses are not conditioned for sale. The owners were not prepared to depart from their homes; hence there might to unwanted items left behind. What is more, the houses might be in a condition worse than regular houses.

Nonetheless, there are still a host of reasons you should look into purchasing a foreclosed home. Below are a few of these reasons:

Bargain Prices

A foreclosed house comes at a price lesser than the original market value. That is the major benefit of buying a foreclosed house. You get real value for your money. Most times the finance houses or owners are eager to get the house off their hands to get back some of their investment as fast as possible. For this reason, the house is usually sold for a reasonable price so there would be a high number of buyers making them offers.

Building Wealth

When you purchase a cheap foreclosure, you can develop wealth. These foreclosed homes which you purchased when the prices were low, can gradually increase in value as the years go by. You will be able to make a decent profit when the time comes for you to sell. You will then be able to channel the profit into other investments which would equally make you wealthier.

However, there is no certainty that the value of the property will go up over the years. But the great part is that, when you purchase a foreclosure at a price lower than the actual value on the market, the chances of its price rising are higher.

Lower Down Payments:

Down payments are very compulsory when purchasing a house through mortgages. These payments must be met without default. Down payment percentages start from 10 percent and above, which makes it a much better bargain.

This, however, is different if you are purchasing your house through foreclosure. Take, for instance, if you are getting a house for the first time through foreclosure; you get to pay less on the down payments when buying them because of the low prices the houses are being sold. This is, however, not the case if it is being bought at the original market value.

Flexible Time Frame

The final closure of a house is not easily determined, and this is due to a range of reasons. Some take days, while others take months, it all depends on the severity of the matter that led to the foreclosure. You can view this as an advantage and not a disadvantage because this provides you ample time to prepare all that is needed by your clients to ensure perfect purchase and agreement.

Dream Neighborhoods

There are times a person's dream house and neighborhood is out of reach because of their inability to finances the purchase of houses in that vicinity. Foreclosure presents an excellent opportunity to purchase houses of your dreams for prices below the original price. This way, you can buy a house at an affordable price and also at your dream location.

Better Financing

When you buy a foreclosed property for flipping, there is a high chance of you getting a good deal for the house. This is because such houses are deemed cheaper than the original price, therefore presenting a good investment opportunity and ensuring you do not need to borrow a large amount for loans, since the property is already coming at a price lower than market value.

It is also better if the foreclosed property is bought directly from the bank or financial institution as the case may be because you can get an up-close negotiated price for the property below what it would have been sold initially for. The reason why it is possible is that the bank or financial houses are usually eager to get the house off the market for a reasonable price without necessarily terming the entire incident as a bad debt leaving you with less closing cost.

External Factors

Real estate is considered lucrative mainly because it can be considered a great investment opportunity and as a result owning a house is a great accomplishment lot of people wish to attain. According to the most recent survey of consumer finances by the Federal Reserve, 65% of Americans are house owners. However, there are a host of external factors that can have an impact on the purchase of properties.

In this chapter, we shall be taking a look at some of these factors and how they can have an impact on your purchase.

Porter's Five Forces

This is an analysis published by Michael E. Porter, in his book *Competitive Strategy: Techniques for Analyzing Industries and Competitors*. He formulated a business analysis model, wherein a company's corporate strategy can be analyzed to identify factors that sustain the company. This is also used to measure the success, rivalry, and appeal of a market or an industry in general. Five common forces that cross over all markets and industries include:

- Power of suppliers

- Power of customers

- Competition in the industry

- Potential new element

- Threat to substitute products.

These five forces listed by porter have the capacity to determine the prices of real estate. For instance, using the third force "'Competition in the industry" if there is a high level of competition in the Real estate industry, prices would certainly go up. All of these external forces have a potential to affect your purchase.

Local Market

No matter the perfection of your property, some factors can depreciate the market price from what it should originally be. For instance, let us assume your property is in the perfect location, in the best condition possible. But in the same area, there are more than three or four houses in the same condition as yours. It will result in a competitive price, therefore affecting the market value of your house. It gives the advantage to interested buyers as there will be a high level of competition. This is called the buyer's market as the person purchasing the house is at an advantage. It will present an opportunity for the buyer to model the contract for the sale of land to his /her advantage. The buyer can make adjustments to the price and make other concessions, such as making repairs. The seller may even have to reduce their purchase price to attract more buyers to the house.

On the other hand, if in the same location mentioned above, your property is the only one in the market and various buyers are interested, it will appreciate the value of your house. This is known to be the seller's market since the seller is at an advantage.

You should also note that the duration at which your house has been put up on the market can also affect the market value of a property. This is called the DOM – that is days on the market.

Demand and Supply

When there is a drastic change in the demographics of a city, there will also be a rise in the requirement for land due to the same reason. When there is a rise in population, it also results in a rise in other economic activities.

The increase in the economic state of a nation directly affects the increase in demand for homes and as such, properties might be considered scarce in environments with high populations because of high demand. This affects the market value of the houses.

A location craze can also lead to a high demand for houses. Take for instance, if Los Angeles is perceived as a city for greener pastures, and as there is an increase in population, it will result in the high demand of land and low supply, which will result to high prices of these houses.

Interest Rates

It is paramount that you make your calculations before rushing to purchase houses. One factor to consider are the interest rates; they can make a house attractive or unaffordable. To be within the right rate, it is advisable to use a mortgage calculator. The role of the interest rate in purchasing a house is a bit tricky; for instance, where the interest rate is low, this will result in the popularity of the house because the mortgage is affordable. This also results in a high market value price.

In reverse, if the interest rate is high, there will be low demand for the house because the mortgage will be deemed unaffordable or expensive. This shares a bit of similarity with bonds. When a value for a bond interest increases, it is deemed affordable and attractive; if it decreases, the value of the bond tends to decrease.

Economic Factors

You can measure the success of an economy by its economic indicators. When an economy is considered excellent, it affects the real estate market. Take, for instance, if there are great employment opportunities, affordable market prices for goods, and production, then the real estate market is affected positively. The effect on real estate can be direct or indirect. If the populace directly controls the object invested in, this might affect the industry widely.

For example, a hotel is a kind of property which has a high level of sensitivity to the activities in the economy. This is because of the lease structure this form of business has. You can see renting a room as a kind of short-term lease because hotel customers can easily avoid them if the economy is not doing well. However, office tenants are usually on a lease which is longer and can't be changed when there is a downturn in the economy. Even though you need to be mindful of the cycle your economy is in, it is also essential that you understand how sensitive real estate property is to the economic cycle.

Legislation Policies

Policies made by legislators can affect the real estate industry to a large extent. It can either boost the inflow of purchase of houses or affect it negatively. If a policy is passed that encourages citizens to purchase houses through incentives, it will boost the real estate company in making more sales. For instance, the United States in the year 2009 witnessed a significant purchase of houses due to the homebuyer's tax credit introduced by the government. According to National Association Realtor the effect of this incentive was quite obvious

Chapter 7: Covering your Bases

The Laws Associated With and Essential Due Diligence Needed For Flipping Properties

Due diligence is all about getting your research done before proceeding to purchase a property. It does not matter what type of home you want to purchase. If you want to cut down on all associated risks, certain things should be done. Ensure that you always carry out an appraisal, as well as the inspection of a property, as it is one of the needed due diligence procedures.

You do not have to end it all here. As a buyer, you can go on with your personal investigation. This section covers all that is involved in due diligence. It also contains due diligence tips that can make real estate transactions successful.

Why Must You Carry Out Due Diligence Yourself?

Although a lot of real estate firms are known to make use of everything at their disposal to carry out due diligence on properties, it is vital that investors carry out due diligence before going ahead to pay for a property. As an individual, you can't bank on what a company does. So, to avoid unnecessary risks, you should carry out due diligence on your own. Before purchasing a property, there are a couple of due diligence items that you have to carry out. They are:

- Ask for an inspection from a home inspector with the right license

- Ask for an appraisal

The Legal Hitches Associated with House Flipping

You really can't tell what the property is about. As a result of this, you have to take zoning, easements, titles, and deeds into consideration.

Due Diligence for Commercial Real Estate

Due diligence for real estate on a commercial scale is different from that for residential real estate. When involved in due diligence for real estate on a commercial scale, the first thing you should do is have a crystal clear reason for purchasing the property. Some popular investor types are:

- Real estate development

- Investment purposes

- Business operations.

The above objective requires different aspects of due diligence. This, therefore, makes it vital that you are fully aware of your reason for buying a property.

Documents That Have To Be Analyzed When Purchasing Commercial Property

When involved in the purchase of commercial real estate, there are many documents that you have to closely look into ahead of making any payments. Getting to know the payment history of tenants, as well as tenant leases, will help you have an idea of what your monthly income from the building will be. This will help you know if purchasing the property is a good enough investment.

Don't stop at tenant leases, look into;

- Zoning regulations
- The title
- The financial records of the seller
- Operating statements
- Tax certificates

Property and Descriptions

Ask for a title report which contains specific details about property liens, and the past owners of the property or easements. As soon as you can gather this, get a professional to survey the property. This will help confirm how accurate the title is.

As soon as the title is certified as accurate, as a buyer, you should go ahead and get title insurance. This will help cover up for unforeseen circumstances.

Is the Property Located in Florida? Ask for a Municipal Lien Search

In Florida, fees, liens, or permits are attached to properties and not individuals. This means a municipal search has to be conducted on every property that is bought in Florida. This is after carrying out a traditional title search.

Sticking to Property and Zoning Codes

Each city, as well as municipality, has its property codes and zoning regulations. Every property has to meet current regulations. To ensure this, you can ask the city for documentation to make sure that no regulation is broken by the property.

While at this, it is preferable that you make use of an independent zoning specialist.

State-Specific ADA Compliance Standards

Find out if the property you are purchasing complies with the Americans with Disability Act (ADA). There are different ADA requirements for various states. To ensure that owners of commercial properties are compliant to ADA regulations in their states, the federal government, as well as ADA makes a checklist available.

Carry Out Due Diligence on the Property Seller

Due diligence is not only carried out on properties, but it is also carried out on the seller of a property. Carry out investigations on the reputation of the seller. Scrutinize such documents as service contracts, prior use of property, loans, prior litigation, etc.

Due Diligence for Lands

When purchasing a piece of land, you need some level of due

diligence. Carrying out due diligence on land is a lot more tasking than doing so on homes. Some due diligence items that are peculiar to purchasing land are covered below.

- **Search the Title**: While searching the title to confirm that the land is not owned by anyone, it is best if you backdate by 30 years. Ensure that you lay your hands on any document with some form of relevance.

- **Put up a General Note for Land Purchase**: Posting a general note for land purchase will help you confirm if the land you are about to buy is indeed free. This is because anyone with information that the land is not free will most likely come forward at this point.

- **Confirm Original Documents of Procurement**: A deed is sometimes regarded as the most vital document everyone interested in buying a piece of land has to take a look at. You can get a deed on the internet and download it after paying a token. If you don't get it from the seller or online, you can do so from a county registry. The deed helps you know the exact place for sale.

- **Get a Professional to Survey the Land**: It is essential to have a land inspection before buying any property. In the absence of boundary lines and land measurement, you should get a surveyor to look into the property. In addition to getting the land measured, a surveyor will help you with all legal descriptions that you need.

- **Ensure Every Property Tax Has Been Paid**: Ask for the official receipts of every property taxes. This way, you can ensure that they have been completely settled by the person that is selling the property to you.

The Authorities: Coping with Ordinances and House Flipping

Here are some overarching authority issues you should get ready for:

- **Permits**: A lot of rehabbers are aware of the existing local regulations as far as permitting new work is concerned. If you are not aware, contact your local government office. A lot of investors are not aware that OLD work which lacked proper permission can lead to issues. Before committing to any property, be in the know.

- **Homeowners Association (HOA):** If you have plans to work on any property that is covered by HOA, you should have the restrictions and covenants at your fingertips.

- **Historic Districts**: Historic districts can severely affect any plans for innovations. Get to find out if your location is part of a historic district.

- **Other Restrictions**: Be careful when you have to work in areas that are protected. Such areas include those that have plants which are regarded as endangered species.

The Checklist

Getting an apartment or house is very exciting and stressful all at the same time. If this is your first flip purchase, it gives you a surreal feeling of ownership and accomplishment, and if you have gotten one before now, you also feel excited about a new place.

In all of these emotions, it is paramount to know how to react in the presence of an estate agent, so you don't give them the advantage of selling the house at an expensive rate and also knowing danger signs to watch out in potential houses.

The following are things to look out for before buying a house;

Roof Condition

You don't necessarily need a degree in the specialization of roof materials before you can tell when the roof is in bad condition. Before looking at what is inside, your observation starts from the outside. Depending on your choice, you might be looking for a new house or a relatively an old house. Your ability to decipher the actual condition of the place is relative to the cost. Therefore, if the roof looks good or bad on the surface, you will be able to tell. The materials of the roof matters too, if a tough material is used to make the roof, it means it is sustainable, if it looks worn out, then in a matter of time, it will cave in and leave you with many repairs.

Look Beyond the Paintings

It is very easy to cover a house with a great choice of color to conceal the true nature of the house. So when inspecting a space, make sure you focus on other things other than the paint, such as appliances and wires. If these things are aging or are loose, then you can tell that the walls are old and the painting will not keep it together for long.

Room Temperature

You do not want to disregard the temperature of the house when you are inspecting potential house choices. This is because structuring a new fireplace, cooling systems or heat system does not come cheap. Old models can be of a grave disadvantage. It is therefore advisable to be mindful of this before choosing your house.

Plumbing Issues

Do not wait until you get a plumber to give an expert opinion before inspecting if plumbing of a house is not in good shape. Carefully check out the toilets, kitchens, and any other section of the house that has a plumbing structure. Look out for molds or leaks or any sort of damage to decipher whether the plumbing is in excellent condition or not.

Your Environment

Your only concern is not just inside the house you want to get but also the environment. Some instances will serve as a deal breaker from getting the house. These could be the likes of gas pollution or an awful sewage system, therefore making the environment inhabitable.

Buy a Well-Insulated House

A well -insulated house will serve as a significant advantage to you. This means that the cooling and heat systems are in excellent conditions. If the windows are double paned, then it means you can successfully shut out the noise from the outside world.

Research the Area

Beyond the house, you must research the environment itself. Some areas are known to be prone to fire, flood, hurricane, or any other natural disasters. It is advisable that you carefully consider your pro and cons before purchasing the house. You don't want to be stuck with an investment that won't bring you any returns.

Look Through All Parts of the Home

Do not consider anything in the house as trivial. Make sure you check everything. Try your hands on the switch, the taps, and the windows, alongside every other thing you can. This way you know what works and what doesn't work and if it would be worth the extra cost later on.

Get An Expert Opinion:

It is advised that you do not make a purchase solely on your own opinion. Even though you have carefully checked everything, you can't authoritatively conclude on the conditions of the apartment. It is thus essential that you engage the services of a professional home inspector who will advise you on the right condition of the house.

Note that a house is not always in the perfect condition; it is only advisable to know to the extent of the damage.

Don't Get Rose Tinted Glasses

Many house flippers or individuals who invest in real estate have a property or a range of properties in their collection they do not want out of their hands. For some, it is partly because they have "fallen for" them due to a sentimental attachment. Maybe the property is just beside the home he/she grew up, or perhaps the investor designed and developed it from scratch.

Irrespective of the reason, the investor or house flipper ends up dwelling on that fact believing buyers would not share their sentiment hence their refusal to sell. This is a trap you need to avoid. You need to let go of emotions when you want to go into flipping of houses. If the numbers do not add up, you need to let go of the property.

Many investors understand that their attachment is not wise. Many of them are glad holding on to these properties even while running losses, hoping that the property would do well in the future.

Sentiments hamper how you invest, and this form of attachment to a property that is not doing well can end up pulling down the performance of your entire portfolio.

How Do You Fix This Issue?

If you are serious about earning money from your investments, you need to avoid this attachment in the first place. You can do this with the methods below:

Categorize Property Strictly As a Financial Responsibility

Have you crunched the numbers? Do they add up? Are the properties you have in your portfolio attaining a capital growth which surpasses the average in your environment? This is a logic you need to apply to any property you invest in. If you are purchasing for the long-term potential, then you will need a reasonable amount of extra capital and personal income.

If you have a property that is not doing well in the medium to short term, you need to consider disposing of it and instead get a property that will offer you equity fast. If you are holding on to a property that is not doing well, your only reason should be to transform it into a personal home later.

Let an Expert Buy the Property for You

This may not seem like an orthodox solution but doing this will ensure you do not fall in love with the property you are buying or make a purchase based on impulse. It also gives you the capacity to make buying decisions using your financial circumstances as opposed to being attracted by things that are not relevant like aesthetics. By working alongside an expert, everything is done with a clear mind as the expert would purchase from a professional perspective.

Use the Sleep Test

Before you decide to buy a new property, ensure you sleep on it first. This eradicates the impulse out of making a purchase.

Review Your Portfolio Frequently

This urges you to be more detached about your property's performance. It forces you not to ignore any property that is not doing well due to attachment.

Chapter 8: Financing

Going into a house flipping business can offer you a great stream of income and the chance to switch careers. Following well-known television shows, it is not difficult to do and spending a lot of time in an elaborate education program is not essential.

However, it is much more difficult than it seems. You need to have technical expertise and the capacity to plan appropriately. However, the major issue most people deal with is perhaps getting finance. You need cash to make cash, so what are your available options for getting the funds? We will be covering all of these in this chapter.

However, before we head on to all of that, how much do you need to flip a house? Let us take a look at the considerations below:

How Much Cash Do You Require To Start A Flip?

Before you go about looking for loans, you need to determine the amount of money you need to begin the flip. There is no one cost fits all when it comes to flipping a home. The final figure tends to vary depending on a few final considerations. These include:

- ARV: ARV or after repair value is an approximation of the price of a property when you are through with the proposed renovations.

- Budget: This is a list of all the possible expenses you would record over a specific period.

- Timeline for Fix & Flip: This is the amount of time you estimate that the process of flipping a home will require. You need to determine this at the start of the project alongside the budget. The timeline begins when you buy the property and ends after you have sold the property.

Once you have determined all of these, you would be able to determine how much it would cost you to flip a property.

Next, let us take a look at your financing options:

Bank Financing

The first location you may want to check for a loan is at the bank nearest to you. Getting loans for flipping houses from banks is similar to attaining any other form of mortgage loan. You will determine the length of the loan, place the required down payment among other essential things.

This may seem pretty straightforward, however attaining a bank loan to flip a home is not always easy. You will require good credit to be applicable for the loan, and the bank might have second thoughts in providing you funding if you have no history of flipping houses successfully.

Line Of Credit

If you have developed equity in your home, it may be a great idea to channel that to finance your house flipping. Home equity loans are basically extra mortgages, and you will be making payment for the loans over a fixed period which is normally with a fixed rate of interest. A home line of credit comes alongside a variable rate, but whenever you need extra finance, you will be able to draw against your credit line.

The major problem you would deal with when utilizing home equity to sort out house flipping deals is that you are placing the home as collateral. If you don't meet up with your line of credit or home equity loan payments, the bank can decide to get your home foreclosed. This can be a huge risk if you are planning to utilize the profits you get from flipping to sort out your loan.

Hard Money Loan

These lenders provide loans for developers or real estate and house flippers on terms a bit different from banks. These loans are created for individuals whose credits are not great but need funds to finish their renovations. These loans are short term, and payment needs to be done between a year and less.

If you are unable to get conventional financing from banks, a hard money loan may be ideal for you. However, it comes with some downsides. The interests in these loans are usually high, and it makes them a very pricey option. What is more, it has a short period of payoff, which means the pressure on you may be high to sell off your flipped home fast to prevent a large payment.

Loan from Family and Friends

Ideally, it's best to avoid mixing money with relationships.

However, this does not imply you should not get loans from a friend or relative. It is less tasking than other loan options, and they have more tendency of providing you with loans at lower rates of interest as opposed to hard money lenders and banks.

If you want to go with this option, it is crucial you put down everything in writing. In doing so, the individual lending you the funds is aware that you plan on holding up your end of the deal.

Real Estate Crowdfunding Sites

This is another option for funding which is rising in popularity. Over the past years, crowdfunding has grown to a well-known method of financing all forms of projects, one of which includes house flipping.

How exactly does this method of finance function? Well, it is quite straightforward. Numerous individuals invest little sums of cash in real estate projects they have an interest in. Those little amounts will be utilized as a source of finance for the project.

Depending on the website utilized, the majority of the crowdfunding investment for flipping homes are either developed as debts or equity.

Equity crowdfunding implies that a part of the property being flipped ends up being purchased by investors. Debt funding, on the other hand, implies that investors buy into a part of a loan or the loan itself.

Use Your Assets

Your assets are great sources of finance. However, most people are not aware of the assets they can utilize. The great news is that; even if you do not have any spare cash lying about, there are other aspects of finance you will be able to find funds.

Where can you find the cash?

- **Credit Cards**: If you own a business or personal credit card, you could equally utilizing it as a means of funding a home you want to flip. This option is only ideal if you will be able to quickly pay off the credit card. This is because they come with interests as high as 18-20 percent.

- **Cryptocurrency**: This digital currency is one traded online and does not have anything to do with banks. If you own cryptocurrencies, you can utilize it to finance your house flipping project. This opportunity is one which is just beginning to gain popularity in the real estate sector. It is most likely going to spread further in real estate during the coming years.

- **IRA**: Another ideal choice could be your IRA or Independent Retirement Account. Even though you are liable to tax penalties if you dip into this before getting to the age of 59.5, the cost does not apply to an individual purchasing a home for the first time. If this is the case, you will be able to loan as much as $10,000 to purchase a home you plan on flipping. However, taking funds from your IRA can hamper its potential for growth moving forward.

- **Self-Directed Solo 401(k)**: This is an incentive plan for retirement channeled to individuals who own a small business and don't have any employees working for you full-time asides from a spouse.

Starting an Online Business for Cash

If you have time on your hands, this can be an excellent option. You can begin an online business to help you raise cash. If you have a sellable skill, then there are numerous opportunities you can take advantage of here.

Some of the options which can help you make money within a reasonable timeframe include:

- Graphics Designer

- Freelance Writer

- Website Developer

- Develop apps and sell them

- Sell pictures

Note that these options are some of the quickest available to you and even these would still take time. If you need financing in haste, then these may not be great options because you still need to work for the money. Also, many them do not give you huge returns and may not be sufficient to finance your house flip completely.

Picking the Best Option

These methods listed above will work if you want to fund your business of flipping houses. Another great thing is that you would be able to combine methods. Irrespective of which method you pick, you have a range of options. Flipping houses is not just for the wealthy, but also for those who are quick-witted. What you need to do is locate the appropriate solution for your distinct requirements.

Formula Needed To See If a Property Will Be Popular

Before you invest in a property, there are a few financial aspects you need to consider. First, you want to estimate the potential of the property to make rental income. You can easily do this by checking out the histories of other properties close to it and assessing the rental histories.

It would also be ideal for gauging if the property will become famous later in the future. For example, if you foresee that you will have the capacity to sell a property at a decent profit later on, then it may be one to consider.

With this information, how do you determine the future value of real estate? Let us use the steps below:

Step 1
You will have to determine your estimated growth rate. According to the U.S. House Price Index, prices of real estate have risen at an average of 3.4% every year since 1991. We will be using it for this calculation and changing this to decimal which would be: 0.034.

To determine the projected future value using your growth rate, you will use this formula:

Future growth = $(1 + \text{annual rate})^{\text{years}}$

You are adding one to the rate and raising it to a power equal to the number of years you have in mind.

Step 2
Next, you multiply this projected growth factor by the present property value. The formula would be:

Future value = (future growth) x (present value)

For instance

Let us assume you purchase a property worth $100,000, and you want to have an estimate of what the value would be in 5 years. Utilizing our average rate of 3.4%, you will be able to calculate the growth factors this way:

Future growth = $(1 + 0.034)^5$ = 1.2

Multiplying this by the present value of $100,000, you will be able to get the property's potential future value:

Future value – 1.2 x $100,000 = $120,000

There you have it. Estimating a real estate investment's future value can be ideal for projecting your potential for profit. However, you need to understand that the worth of the property may not be worth this amount exactly. This should only serve in calculating estimates.

Chapter 9: Formulas You Need To Keep In Line

For anybody interested in house flipping, there are a few things you need to learn even before you make an offer or even approach a lender. Even if you have once purchased a home, the same rules don't apply when it has to do with investment. Investment in properties is all about the numbers.

If you plan on being successful in the business of flipping houses, you need to utilize and understand some formulas which would help you make decisions. All of these formulas are based on the figures and once you determine them, getting financing for flipping your first home would be easy.

Now, let's check out some of the critical formulas you need to learn:

ARV or After Repair Value Formula

The ARV is an estimate of the future cost of a property after undergoing repairs. After repair value is not the present value of a property after buying. Instead, it is the value of the property after enhancements have been made.

There are a lot of factors that can have an impact on the ARV calculation. However, it consists of two major aspects which are the value of repairs and purchase price of the property.

The formula for ARV is: (Purchase Price of Property) + (Cost of Renovations)

70% Rule Formula

According to this rule, you need to purchase a property/home at 70% of the ARV deducted from the cost of repairs.

Maximum purchase price = (ARV X 70%) - cost of repair

Formula for Maximum Purchase Price

After using the rule above to analyze how valid a deal is, you can use this formula in carrying out an elaborate analysis of the overall costs in the project.

The formula for this is: ARV – Holding costs – Repair costs – selling costs – funding costs – profit = Maximum Purchase Price

Formula for Expected Return on Investment

This is the amount you are expecting to make after flipping a home. The more your return on investment, the more your profit. This is what everyone in the business aims for. The lower your return on investment, the less profit you get. The ARV, timeline, and budget all have an impact on your ROI.

To calculate this, use this formula:
ROI = Net Profit / Overall Investment x 100

Formula for calculating offer price

To calculate the offer price, use the formula below:
ARV – (Cost of renovations + Holding and closing costs + profit target +financing cost) = Offer price.

Chapter 10: Renovating

Ensuring a home is adequately fixed can bring in a decent amount of revenue when you want to sell. Most times, buyers search for homes that need minimal repairs, and you won't want to lose a deal because there were problems the buyers could not deal with right? A little bit of fixing can save you from this hassle.

This chapter will focus on the critical things to repair in a property before a sale. This is to avoid spending so much money on repairs that are not important or will not make so much difference.

The following are areas you should consider when repairs are to be made in a property with the aim of selling. They include:

Bathrooms and Kitchen

These parts of the house are considered the most technical. This is because it involves a lot of mechanical work, such as electrical and plumbing works. Therefore, it is prone to faster damage than others. When considering repairs check out the following:

- **Kitchen Appliance:** Look out for any leaks in the fridge or freezer. Also, make sure that appliances such as microwave or dishwashers are in a working condition.

- **Cabinets:** Fix any loose hinges in any cabinet doors and drawers, replace broken handles and knobs.

- **Sinks, Faucets, and Showers:** There should not be

leakage in the bathtub or the kitchen. Make sure that the faucets and showers in the bathroom are equally in excellent conditions. Replace them if there is any damage.

- **Bathtubs:** Ensure drains are functional. If the acrylic is coming off on a bathtub, you could replace it or resurface the tub.

Home Interiors

It is essential to take a good look at the home interior of the house, such as:

- **The Walls and Ceilings**: where there is discoloration due to water damage, that space should be repainted. Watch out for any dents on the wall or holes are and fix any you find.

- **Flooring**: make sure any broken tiles are repaired and replace any worn out or torn carpets. If the layout is a carpet, make sure it is neat and clean.

- **Heating, Ventilation, Air Conditioning, and Water Heater**: All aspects of these should be working correctly. Make sure the thermostat is fully functional. It is paramount that there is no leak and they should be clean.

- **Detectors:** Your smoke and carbon monoxide detectors should not be less than nine years old. If they are its best to replace them; make sure they are functioning correctly.

- **Electrical Panels and Circuit Breakers:** It is

paramount that these are up to date and they correspond with the current codes. If you cannot figure when to go about it, make sure you call in an electrician to do the job, if it is an old model, then, make sure it is checked.

Home Exterior

One of the important places you would want to make some changes to is the exterior of the property. Below are some of the core parts:

- **Roof:** Inspect the roof closely and make sure it is in excellent condition, look out for any water damage, holes, or cracks in the sealant. No tiles should be misplaced or broken. Also, look out for ridge caps that are missing and shingles that are broken. Make sure they are all fixed.

- **Drainage**: A strong foundation is essential for a home. This can be weakened if the drainage system is faulty, as a result of the collection of water on the foundation. Get a professional that can aid in redirecting the drainage to the proper route.

- **Eaves:** It is vital that the eaves are not damaged by water or rutty. Make sure you replace the affected area or involve a professional.

- **Garage doors:** This should be in an excellent working condition. There should not be any dents and dings. The security system should meet with the local codes requirements.

Yards:

- **Fencing**: If the model of your fence is wood or metal, make sure it is not termite damaged or rusty, but smooth. Get a professional or do it yourself by scrubbing the fence or making use of a rust converter. Prime the affected area and then paint.

- **Landscaping:** Your landscape area should be clean, and your vegetation should not touch the house.

- **Decks**: Where the deck is damaged by termites or water, it is vital that it is repaired. The patio should be in good condition with code compliant guardrails, including the support columns. As a measure of precaution, apply polyurethane on the patio or deck.

DIY vs. Contracting

When you get a property you want to renovate, you have the option of either doing it yourself or paying someone to do the work. This chapter aims at pointing out the factors to consider while determining if you should do the job yourself or get a general contractor.

Getting a Contractor

Engaging a general contractor is well worth it; they are known to be experts in the field and can make decisions that are beneficial to you. For example, if you want to restructure a room, or merge two rooms. He/she will be able to tell if this is possible or it might result in damage to your property.

They will generally oversee the entire project from start to finish without delay because it is their primary duty to make sure the job is well done. The project is likely to be done right on time, as opposed to DIY where you try and correct mistakes multiple times before it is done perfectly well.

Another considered advantage of involving a general contractor is their ability to have a financial plan, which can sustain the project until the end. They can map out how much materials will cost and how much the laborers will be paid and how long the project will take before it is finished. All of these are possible because of their experience in the field.

As an expert, a contractor is well informed on the permits you require to engage in specific home renovations. This will save you from issues with the authorities, as the property owner is deemed at fault and not the contractor if you fail to get the required permit. A contractor can also decipher which area of the jobs they can be involved in without a permit. This way, there is progress on the project.

Choosing a General Contractor

It is advisable to conduct an interview with potential contractors. This way you can determine what is generally accepted in the field and their knowledge. Before the interview, inform them that their portfolio and referees are required for the interview.

During the interview, take into consideration how fast they arrived at the interview. Also, note if they were organized and if they were so busy they had to change interview schedules regularly. After the interview it is essential you go through the references they stipulated and other customers they had previously worked for.

You can go a step further by visiting the site they had previously worked on. After a contractor has been chosen, it is crucial you are aware of the person's financial status. It is important because, a general contractor might need to urgently get materials without waiting on you, being fully aware that you will reimburse them. There are also scenarios where they will have to pay off the laborers employed by them before the check comes in.

Negotiating With Contractors

If you want to have a successful negotiation with a contractor, it is best to tailor the conversation in a way that won't feel like a negotiation. Whenever you haggle over a service someone is specialized in, you need to try to find a way to suggest to the seller you want a discount without sounding rude. You don't want an unsatisfied and pissed contractor looking for methods of cutting corners while working on your project to make up for what he believes is an unfair price.

Let's talk about the three effective strategies you can use for a successful negotiation with a contractor.

Let Him Know You Are Getting Numerous Bids.

Having more than one bid for your property puts you at an advantage because you can tell your contractor that there are other bidders without having to lie. This sends a message to the contractor:

- Price is a concern to you

- There are other contractors who are interested in the same project
- He needs to step up and provide you with his best price

This does not mean the contractor with the lowest bid should always be your option; instead, hire a contractor that offers the best services and has a good reputation. However, by competing for your business, all the parties involved are sure to offer better prices.

Request His Input

Your contractor may pick offense if you out rightly ask for a reduction in their charge. Rather than doing so you can ask your contractor for suggestions on how you can cut down the cost to meet your demand. If for instance his bid is $25,000 and you can only afford to pay $20,000 ask him if any changes could be done to bring down the cost.

He might suggest you go for a less expensive but quality flooring or a different design for your kitchen that would bring down the cost yet give you the best. Asking for opinions on what areas to cut down you find his input valuable reduces the tendency of offending the contractor. This would also lay more emphasis on how tight your budget is, which might prompt him to find other ways to cut down cost.

Add Your Expertise

If you are less busy and have experience in DIY, you can do a few parts of the project yourself to save some money. By so doing you can request that the contractor cuts down his price a bit. For instance, you can fix the broken fence and put the landscaping in order by yourself which should bring about a decrease in charges. You can also look around and figure out other areas you can correctly take care of and get right to. It could be excavation work, basic demolition or even painting of the property. Doing any of these by yourself can result in a decrease in the price of the project which puts hundreds or thousands of dollars back in your pocket.

Home Renovation DIY

DIY is cheap and sometimes considered therapeutic, but before you engage in renovating a house, you must be sincere yourself and answer the following questions:

- Are you skillful for the kind of result you desire?
- Are you a busy person? Do you have the time?
- Do you have sufficient information on how to carry out the project?
- Can you exercise patience when needed?
- Do you have the finances to furnish the project for as long as it goes?
- Are you capable of finishing the project?

If the answer is negative, it is advisable you reconsider your decision of doing the project yourself. You must also realize that you need experts during a renovation, such as electricians, architects, and the likes. It only means you have the responsibility of hiring a great worker who is qualified in handling the job. You must also make yourself available to make decisions when needed.

Split The Work:

Another alternative is where you split the work between yourself and a general contractor. This way you will handle projects that are less demanding and assign the rest to the contractor. It is paramount that you clearly define your responsibility from that of the contractor to avoid conflict.

Quick Fixes

Sometimes, when you purchase a property, it may be difficult to identify most of the wear and tear. However, the moment you decide to sell, things become more evident. You begin to identify the flaws that need to be fixed, but you have limited resources and not enough time to get them all fixed. Then, what aspects do you fix to make quick cash?

The best way to get more money off your property is by fixing the crucial things that need fixing before putting up the property for sale.

Let's take a look at some of the quick fixes you can make before listing a property.

Paint

Paint is one of the most affordable ways to improve the look of your home. The good thing is you can do it yourself. There are videos online that would help you do a perfect job. Neutral colors appeal better to people and are therefore better for homes up for sale. This gives room for the potential buyer to visualize how they want their home to be.

Rooms with dark or dirty paints should be painted while those that are still appealing to the eyes can be left out. All wallpapers are best removed to maximize profit. Wallpapers are most times unattractive to buyers, but a good number of sellers are ignorant of these. They sometimes assume the buyer will overlook it, but they rarely do. Leaving the wallpapers until the buyer requests for it to be taken down defeats the purpose of making a good profit.

Exterior

The first thing a buyer sees is the exterior of the home. For this reason, it must look its best. Fix the fence if broken, clear out unnecessary items littering the yard or the garage.

Ensure the landscaping is in perfect order and good looking. You can go the extra mile to beautify the surroundings by planting colorful flowers.

Kitchen

Having a spacious kitchen with modern appliances is the desire of most people, this raises the need to upgrade the appearance of your kitchen. However, do not make the mistake of doing a complete renovation without the assurance of recovering the money.

Little touches here and there can do the magic but do not go beyond your renovation budget. You can paint the kitchen walls and change old or damaged appliances. In recent times, the cost of solid surface materials has dropped so you might consider installing any within your reach.

Bathroom

It is imperative that your bathroom has all its appliances in good working condition. Fix whatever needs to be fixed and better still, replace if you can. This would give your bathroom a better look and leave potential buyers impressed.

Make your bathroom look as clean and bright as possible. You can achieve this by taking down old wallpapers and repainting the room.

The two most crucial areas in a home are the bathroom and kitchen, and they are also the most expensive to upgrade. Therefore, you need to do what's possible to make these areas look their best.

Lighting

The effect of lighting in a property should not be underestimated. Lighting will make your home look spacious even if it's a lot smaller. There are various styles of lighting you can find online that would best suit your property and give it the look potential buyers will desire.

Refinishing Hardwood Floors

Without a doubt, the most common flooring in most homes is the hardwood floors. Wood floors have a look that can give your home a unique appearance, and this is the most preferred kind of flooring for most buyers. This means that if you must get the best off your property, it is advisable to do a refinishing for your hardwood floors.

Outside Revamp

You are now at the period where you want to sell the house. However, even to you, it does not look as appealing and modern as it should be right from outside. The great news is that there are several ways you can improve the exterior look of your property to make it more appealing to the eyes. This may include changing the landscaping.

The improvements discussed in this chapter are very affordable and not time-consuming. The best part of it is that they give your home a new and modern look you and your prospective buyers can't help but admire.

Use Outdoor Lighting

Lighting up your entryway gives your home a better look at night and most of all increases safety, especially for visitors. It also makes your home more welcoming and has a way of bringing out the beauty of your landscaping and other amazing features of your home. The lights reduce the dark areas in and around your home making it safer.

The best form of lighting for sidewalks and paths are the solar lights that do not require electrical cables. Also, they are easy to install and do not function using the house electricity. Solar lights run for a limited time which has been estimated to be for at least six hours.

Take Advantage of Gravel

The use of gravel can help you achieve that look you desire for your driveway. There is an unexplainable feeling that comes with the sound tires make on gravel. Simply pour gravel on any area of your home you wish to beautify. But you must have in mind that it is a little difficult to maintain gravel as you need to rake often to stop the gravel from spreading into where it is not wanted.

Edge the Driveway

Your driveway will look a lot more fabulous when you install border along it. You can make use of different edging materials like stones, bricks pavers or a combination of any to get the desired look. Although the edging can be made to be on the same level as the driveway, it is best to make it a little higher to prevent driving into the lawn.

Plant Flowers

Do you wish to improve your curb appeal? If yes then plant flowers. Plant flowers wherever necessary to add more beauty to your home. Raised garden beds, flowers along the sidewalk, inside flower boxes, or in front of the house can give your home a fantastic appearance. Flowers are very affordable and require less effort to plant and maintain. They also give your home a fantastic look.

To maximize the effect of flowers in your home beautification, it is best to consult your local nursery for a recommendation on the kind of flower that would thrive in your home. Planting perennial plants will save you the stress of cultivating new flowers yearly.

Construct a Berm

Building a berm gives you the room to add color to your yard. It could be through flowers, trees, stones or mulch. You can as well make use of flagstone or pavers to create an excellent looking edging. Most berms are soft with curving edges which allows you to create something unique off it.

The processes involved in developing a berm is similar to that of a garden. First, you clear the grasses, fertilize the soil and then finally plant your trees or foliage. Add rocks, mulch or edging to make it look beautiful.

Cover up Dead Spots

Most perennial trees take up all the nutrient in the soil. Their shades also prevent the grasses from getting sunlight which hinder their growth and eventually leading to their death. The areas with dead grasses become unappealing to the eyes. To combat this and save yourself some stress, plant flowers that thrive well under shades around the lawn. This will drastically improve the look of the landscape.

A much easier solution is to apply mulch around the base of the tree. Your surrounding will look a lot better if you cover the dead areas. Applying mulch around the base of the tree helps reduce the loss of moisture needed by the root. However, applying too much would encourage the breeding of pests and possibly suffocate the root of your tree which may result in death. The perfect quantity of mulch needed to achieve the desired result is not more than 2 inches.

Chapter 11: Sell That House

Increasing the Value of the Property

It is only reasonable that you would want to get the most you can from a property. A property's value is majorly centered on the location, the neighborhood, the building structure, functionality, and its aesthetic layout. Some of these factors are not within your control, for example, the neighborhood. There are however factors that are within your control, the result of which will increase your property value to a reasonable percentage which you can change today.

Doing this will ensure the sale of your property is fast for the top price available. Below are some ways you can enhance the value of your property:

Clear-up Your Garden

As they say, the first impression lasts long. Your ability to increase the value of your home and attract potential buyers starts from the first look they get of the house. The first part of your property buyers view is the exterior which includes your garden.

It is essential that the garden looks good, but you do not have to spend so much money to achieve this, all you need is some soil and decorative features to create a good look and draw in those serious buyers.

Clear Out Excess Litter

For a potential buyer to take an interest in the house, it is vital that they can visualize the space and make it their own. This might be impossible if you still have some of your belongings littered around. It is therefore advisable you create a great space in every compartment of the house. This gives the house aura of neatness and a more extensive space and consequently gives the house a reasonable price tag.

Make Repairs

It is vital that you do not leave the house in bad condition. Making even simple repairs like fixing the kitchen or bathroom sink or replacing rotted wood all have the capacity to enhance the value of your home. These repairs won't cost much, since they are not major, but they would make a huge difference when it is time to sell.

Use Paint To Your Advantage

Painting the property gives it a fresh, appealing look. Especially if you make good use of beautiful color. It is crucial you do not use excessively loud colors as your potential buyers might not want this. It is advisable to make use of neutral colors. The advantage of this is that they can fit in their imagination of what they want the apartment to look like. Another advantage of using a neutral color is that it gives the space a broader and more spacious look.

Make Replacements:

Look around the house for things that are not working correctly and fix them. It is essential you take into consideration the doors and windows; if faulty, make sure they are replaced or repaired. Your potential buyer is likely to jump into a conclusion that the house is in bad condition just because your doors and windows are not working correctly. Avoid such impression by doing the needed repairs.

Kitchen Makeover

For most homes, the kitchen is the center of family life. It gives the house homely feel. It is therefore essential that the kitchen is fully functional and looks great. This is not to increase your expenses but to increase the value of the property. You do not have to change the entire kitchen; few repairs here and there can help in giving the kitchen a warm and welcome look

Clean Bathroom

Most individuals including potential buyers will be displeased and perhaps turned off by dirty bathrooms. Having a bathroom with a strong and unappealing stench. On the property you want to sell is not welcoming. It also sends a message that the entire house is dirty and not habitable. It does not take so much to make a bathroom clean. Make some changes if need be, such as the sinks or toilets, and make repairs where needed.

Make Your Property Ready For Use

Create an impression that your house is ready to be moved into at any time. This is mostly appreciated by potential buyers who are just getting their home for the first time. Your ability to pull this off will undoubtedly increase the value of the house. All you need to do is make sure, the garden, the rooms, bathrooms, kitchen, garage are cleared out, neat and repaired.

Include Furniture

Sometimes, the fastest way to sell your property for a high-value cost is to show the potential buyers what the house can look like if they move in. To achieve this, you have to set the place at its finest. It will involve good paint, furniture layout, and a beautiful kitchen. You do not necessarily have to own any of these furniture. You can merely loan the furniture and after the sale, return them.

Get A Good Real Estate Agency

A fast way of getting your property off the market is engaging the services of a great real estate agent. They will be able to present your property to potential buyers in an attractive way.

Please note that in renovating the house, you need to be cautious with your spending. It is advisable to do the needful only and nothing else. This is just because you might be dipping into the profit you would make from the property in renovating. Ensure you consider your after repair value while renovating. That way you can adequately get an excellent price for your property.

Attracting Buyers

Let us assume you have correctly done all you need to sell off your property quickly. You've tried to make the house attractive by clearing the garbage and making the surrounding beautiful, yet you find it difficult to get a generous buyer as quickly as you expected.

This is a common experience and could be very annoying and frustrating. But, the good thing is there are still a few things you can do to attract buyers. Below we shall talk about a few more things would help you attract the perfect buyer for your home as quickly as possible.

Know the Selling Point of the Property

If you desire to sell off your investment property as quickly as possible, then it is highly necessary to know what makes your home unique. What attracted you to the house at first? This could be the selling point of that house. You can ask for the help of a real estate agent if you have trouble identifying the uniqueness of the property.

Offer a Reasonable Price

It is very crucial to choose the right price if your property must be sold quickly; a real estate agent can help you fix a perfect price for your property. A lot of people believe using the services of a realtor will cost more money, but it's not always so. There are certain valuable services a realtor offers and this is one of them.

Avoid the temptation of placing your property at a very high cost. This is because an overpriced property will take a much more extended period to get off the market and might depreciate in value, eventually being sold at a lower price.

Take Advantage of the Web

Do not rely solely on the listing of your agent; make use of other online platforms to market your property. You might eventually get the right buyer on one of these platforms like Zillow.com or trulia.com.

When listing your property on the web, ensure you take great pictures. Nobody is going to purchase a property with shoddy pictures. The picture has to be bright and appealing enough to get them to stop to see what you are offering.

Organize an Open House

Organizing an open house is an excellent way to advertise your home sale. Make adverts for the open house by placing signs all around your environment. Ensure there is some light refreshment. Also, place brochures regarding the home which visitors can pick up as they head out.

Show Your Home

If you are on the property during the day, you will be able to show the home on your own. If this is not the case, you need to be ready to keep a key in the lock box and respond to calls from other buyers an agent. Note that you have to be sure of the agent's identity before you offer the combination of the lock box.

Another great option you can use is to get the services of an a la carte real estate agent to help you with it at a price. Once the agent is through showing your home, you need to follow up with calls as regards feedback.

Negotiate and Close

When it comes to closing a house flipping deal, there are various aspects you need to take a close look at if you want to get the most from a sale.

They include:

Negotiation

When a buyer provides you an offer on your property, you can either:

- Accept the terms without changes
- Counteroffer with modifications
- Reject the offer

Counteroffers are the most common. It is like a back and forth between potential buyers and yourselves. If you observe that their prices are not moving or moves slowly, you would have to either reject or accept their price.

When negotiating, ensure your emotions don't take over and ensure it remains strictly business. The instant you sign a contract, you will still need them before you close and you don't want to have to deal with a buyer you were not kind to before.

If you have more than one offer, you can take advantage of this. Tell each buyer you want a better offer and he who provides the best, is the one you would sell to. Set up a timeframe for when you would pick the top offers. Someone who wants to purchase the property will respond fast.

Ensure you are not hasty during the process of negotiation. However, you need to ensure it does not drag for too long either. This part of the process should not take beyond three days under ideal circumstances. If it takes more time than that, your buyers may no longer have an interest in the property and move on. Ensure you place all agreements in writing and ensure that every party involved pens his/her signature.

Closing

Simply put, this is when the buyer pays the seller to get the property deed. Both sellers and buyers need to attend this with their real estate agents, their attorneys if needed, alongside a closing agent.

If you are not bringing an attorney, ensure you get all the documents you need to close beforehand. Ensure you review all the documents comprehensively. You need to understand what you agree to by signing.

You need to be polite to your closer. This is because they can make the process of closing extremely difficult or easy. The title company will equally have the responsibility of recording the property deed with the local government. They will also record the mortgage of the buyer with the bank.

The process of closing can take a lot of time for sellers if the properties are not prepared. You need to get the most you can beforehand. Knowing what to anticipate will ensure this experience is seamless for all parties and that you get as much as you can get from the deal. After all of these have been done, you can then celebrate all of your efforts. Negotiations between you and the buyer will begin when a buyer makes an initial offer. Note that depending on the state you reside in, this stage may differ. Ensure you ask your agent to break down everything in detail. Ensure you don't sign a contract till you are particular about everything in the offer and how you will be affected.

Closing the Deal

The sale of a home is perhaps one of the essential aspects of a house flipping business. The choices you make when agreeing with the buyer on a price can have a considerable effect on the amount of cash you earn on your investment.

These techniques below can help you make top dollar on your investment.

Counter at Your List Price

Buyers always anticipate some haggling so their starting offer would not be as high as your list price. However, it would also be less than what they plan on paying.

This is the period many sellers will counteroffer using a price less than their list price because they are scared of losing a sale. They desire to seem willing and flexible to head into negotiations and close the deal. This is an effective strategy if you want to sell the property; however, if you want to make the most cash, it is not the way to go.

As opposed to reducing your price to get close to the offer of the buyer, you need to offer a counter at your list price. Anyone who has an interest in making a purchase will offer you higher. If you started your property at a reasonably high price, when you counter with your list price, it makes it evident that you understand the value of your property and you have the intention of attaining your deserved cash.

This strategy will surprise many buyers, and a few of them will be put off because you don't want to negotiate and leave. However, this will also ensure you don't waste time on those buyers who make only very low offers and are more interested in attaining a bargain as opposed to purchasing your property.

Do not accept the offer

This is a more extreme strategy as opposed to the first. All you do is reject the offer from the buyer without countering. To ensure they stay engaged, you can request they send in another offer. If they genuinely have an interest, they will send in another offer.

This technique passes a more powerful signal that you are aware that your property is worth what you are requesting. Any buyer who sends in another offer will need to increase his offer.

Additionally, by not countering, you are not engaged in a negotiation with a specific buyer. This ensures you will be able to accept an offer which is higher if it comes. On the other hand, when the buyer is aware that another person can make an offer which is better than his at any time, he/she will be under pressure to quickly send in a competitive offer if they have an interest in the home. This strategy is beneficial if you have not placed the property on the market for a long time or you are about to have an open house soon.

Try to Start a Bidding War

Get your property listed on the market and ensure it is available for showing. After a few days, set up time for an open house. Do not agree to entertain offers till the open house is over. You may want to contemplate on holding an open house which is not as popular like the broker's preview.

Prospective buyers will anticipate competition, and as a result of this, they might increase their offers. You may not get more than a single offer, but the buyer won't be aware. However, if you get more than one offer, you can head to the peak bidders and request that they make their best and highest offer.

Let Your Counteroffer Have an Expiration

When a buyer sends in an offer that you don't find suitable, you will be able to counter this offer. When you do this, you become involved in a negotiation with the other party that is legally binding, and you won't be able to accept any other offer that comes along even if it a better one.

If you want to sell your home on time, you can add a brief expiration time when sending your counteroffer. This is a strategy that urges the buyer to make up his/her mind, so you will either be able to move on or place your property under contract.

Ensure the deadline is not extremely short so you don't turn off buyers. However, you need to try making it less than your state's standard real estate contract time frame. If the default number of days for expiration is four days, make yours 2 or 3 days.

Asides from quickly closing the deal, you have another reason to urge sellers to get to a decision on time. When you have an outstanding counteroffer, your home is not on the market. Many buyers won't send in an offer when there is an ongoing negotiation. However, if the deal goes through, you would have included additional time to the number of days your property has remained on the market. The higher the number of days your home remains on the market, the lower the level of appeal it has, and the higher your likelihood of reducing your asking price to find a buyer.

To execute these strategies for negotiation successfully, your product or property has to be of excellent quality. The home needs to be in excellent condition and offer what other properties do not offer especially if you want an edge in negotiations. If the property you are offering does not trigger excitement in a buyer, all of your tactics would only result in them walking away.

When No One Is Buying

For many individuals involved in house flipping, they must probably have asked themselves or heard someone ask them the dreaded question: Why is my house not selling?

In some situations, the answer may be evident. In others, the reason is not very clear.

As an investor in real estate or house flipper, your most dreaded situation is the inability to get a buyer for your home. What happens if you make renovations, place it on the market, and strike all the right boxes but yet, no one shows interest? Thinking about it may be discouraging; however, it does happen.

If you find that your home is not selling after being listed for more than three months, below are the steps you can take to rectify this issue:

Utilize High-Quality Pictures

This may be obvious to some. However, numerous sellers miss this point. Let us assume you are the buyer. If you check out a property listed online without pictures, there is a high probability you just went past without thinking twice right?

Pictures are crucial to a listing. This is why it is essential to use the best pictures you can. If you are unable to do it yourself, get the services of a professional. The additional cash and time will undoubtedly be worth it.

Advertise Your Listings in Additional Locations

Sometimes, the calls you want coming in won't come until you advertise on numerous platforms. Imagine this: out of 2,000 people; there may be only one buyer who has an interest in for your property. What this means is that you need to ensure as many people as possible see your listing if you plan on meeting serious buyers.

In many situations, you are most likely not going to get it if you place an ad on one platform and move on with your life like nothing is happening. You need to place your ad on as many platforms as you can. Do not stop! Let as many individuals as possible come across your ad.

Increase the Frequency of Your Promotion

When you are working with sites like eBay, Craigslist, and Classifieds where ads are pushed off the front page fast, it is essential you renew these ads frequently if you plan on remaining in front of individuals.

If you don't try as much as you can to ensure your information is on the top of every list, many people would not see it. It is just the way it is. Speaking factually, many buyers including myself won't head to the 40th page to view your listing.

If you are unable to get your ad to the center or front, many people won't see your ads. You need to ensure you are remaining at the top of the listings whenever you can.

Enhance the Property

Irrespective of the kind of house you are trying to flip, there is the possibility that somebody out there would gladly pay above the price you are asking for or higher if it came with one extra feature. The concept is to determine what this feature would be.

You may want to go all the way and attach an automatic garage door, or perhaps install a smart system. You could as well do something trivial like adding better fixtures to the bathroom.

Reduce the Price

Sometimes this is the least difficult thing to do. However, it is not something you want to do in a hurry. Reducing the price is not difficult because you don't need to overthink. In many scenarios, it will ensure you sell faster, but it can easily lead to a loss on your part.

Because it is not difficult to reduce your price does not imply it is the best step for you to take. Yes, it is possible that your asking price is excessive because it does not have the value. However, there are numerous instances where you will be able to dispose of your property for your asking price. This is only a reality if you locate the appropriate buttons and use to your benefit.

If you can focus on ensuring your buyers to see the value, you will observe that many people will gladly pay your full price if they believe that they are attaining value in the surplus amount that you are requesting they pay.

Keeping the Property for Rent

Renovating a property and selling it off is as profitable as renting it out. Any of the strategies would work fine. All you need to do is evaluate your objectives for the investment. Compare the pros and cons of these strategies and choose the one that best works for you depending on your budget and plans.

Market Factors

The amount of profit that would be realized from a property will determine if it would be flipped or rented out, but the market factor plays a significant role in the profitability of either option. It is always less challenging to acquire a house than to sell when there is a crash in the market even if the house has been improved to a higher standard.

This means that if the number rented property in your neighborhood supersedes the number of renters, holding on to your property for a rental might be a bad idea. You could end up spending more money paying for mortgages while waiting for someone to rent. Therefore, you need to evaluate your environment and the market before deciding on what to do with your property. In this case, flipping becomes a better option than renting.

Renting Benefits and Drawbacks

If you have tenants, putting up your property for rental will be a better and quicker source of income, but only as long as the property is in excellent condition. Your rental price will be determined by what others in the neighborhood are charging for something similar to your property. If your property is overpriced when compared to other similar properties, it becomes challenging to find renters unless you bring down the price which might affect you.

However, the value of property keeps changing and might eventually come up to your stipulated price and play out in your favor. It takes considerable work and effort, and not everyone is cut out for such stress. If you, however, want to retain your property as a rental but can't handle the work involved, you might want to consider hiring a rental manager to help you out. This means you get to spend more while paying for the services of a rental manager.

Calculating Rental Earnings

After proper analysis and if you realize buying a property for rental would be futile and a waste of time and effort, then there is no need acquiring such property. Making a list of the expenses that come along with a property can help you determine how profitable the property would be if rented out. Some of these expenses include annual cost such as mortgage fees if you are paying for the property; property taxes, insurance, utilities, and maintenance on the home; advertising, and vacancy factor or the period when there wouldn't be a tenant or occupant of the property.

You should also put into consideration the vacancy factor utilized by mortgage lenders and real estate agents, which is usually at 5%. To determine the monthly cost, divide the total annual cost by 12 and then compare it with the amount you desire to charge. The outcome of this should influence your decision.

Chapter 12: The Do's and Don'ts

When Things Go Wrong

Even the most successful house flippers had to start from scratch. They had to make errors, made changes, tried again, and won. One of the essential traits which make the experienced professionals different from the starters is that when things go wrong, they see it as a lesson. All failures are ways to learn something new, and the best in the field never forgo an opportunity to learn something new.

See All Failures as Opportunities

Flipping homes can be a great way of grounding yourself in the real estate industry. Although it can be quite annoying and tedious at the start, when you make use of the proper practices and systems, you will begin to make adequate returns on your investments in no time.

However, it is vital to understand that when you invest in properties, you need to do it using actual figures instead of hope and emotion. This does not mean the process can't be fun or enjoyable, but you need to ensure you don't become too attached.

Having said that, what do you do if your plan does not go how you anticipated?

The only way to obtain success in the business of house flipping is if you can see how valuable failure can be. You need to understand that sometimes you have to take a hit; take a few steps backward, use the lesson you learned, and come up with a better plan to ensure success.

It may seem cliché to state that failure does not exist, but in the case of house flipping, this statement is accurate. That being said, you may want to make all the mistakes you can in your first house. When you begin with hits from scratch, you will have no option than to go further.

When Should It Be Appropriate To Walk Away?

As we covered earlier, failure is valuable. However, you need to have an excellent strategy for an exit. If you find out that you have made a terrible investment choice and you seem to be making no headway, then it may be ideal to walk away instead of holding on to a loss.

At times, the best decision you can make is to sell the property even if it is at a price lower than what you anticipated. If you can break even and get a little loss, it would be a better decision than keeping a property with the hopes of selling it in the future. Doing this will leave you responsible for the clearing of any loans that have to do with the property. You will also be in charge of any extra costs that come with it as well.

So if you are unable to get the price you desire, it may be the right time for you to cut your losses and walk away. Then you can channel your energy into investing in more profitable properties.

Ongoing Mindset

When it has to do with flipping houses alongside other self-operated businesses, mindset makes a lot of difference. A successful house flipper would not think similarly as the employee of an organization. There are some essential skills to have.

First, if you want to be successful in the house flipping business, you cannot blame other factors or individuals when a deal fails to go as you wish. Doing this does not seem professional and always results in problems. You need to always be ready to take responsibility for the outcomes of your actions. If you blame the investors, clients or market, you will always fall into problems. By taking responsibility, you will place yourself in a position for new opportunities.

You also need to learn from the success and mistakes of others. Some more experienced hands in the business have made issues and always share, so other people don't fall in the same traps. You need to take advantage of this and always be willing to learn from those who have attained more success in the field.

Many experts and television shows will try to make it seem flipping houses is an easy and fast way of making wealth; this is not wrong. To be successful anywhere you need to be ready to work hard for it, and house flipping is not different. Overnight success does not exist, and you need to be committed through the bad and good times if you want to be successful.

If you want to be successful in the house flipping or real estate business, or any other one for that matter, you must develop a persistent mentality to always keep learning. This is a mindset that one must groom and understand if they want to be successful in this business. Many successful house flippers have a broad range of skills which is due to their desire for knowledge.

There is something that successful real estate investors and house flippers do, and that is to learn continuously. They all have the desire to learn. As one who is just going into the business, it may be hard to take a few steps back to learn something new during a busy day. But, it is essential for you to find the time every day to broaden you're the knowledge you have of the real estate business. The ongoing learning mindset is one that can be of benefit and push you throughout your time in the business. It is one that should never end.

Although learning is crucial, you need to also be able to change with the times and improve yourself as well continually. Learning from the mistakes you make can help you succeed. When you admit that you don't know everything and you learn every day, you are on the path to being successful. Many experts in the field pick up on their past mistakes, and instead of categorizing it as a failure, they take them as lessons. You need to learn to do this as well. You will have to learn to use the experience you had in the past as a way to point out what you did not do correctly and how to ensure it does not happen again. Sometimes, mistakes lead you to new openings.

To be successful in the game of flipping houses, it needs a unique sort of mindset. An ongoing learning mindset for success will consist of an unwavering desire to take risks and learn. The road to success is not easy, and if you want to be financially free, flipping houses can help you achieve that goal.

Common Mistakes

So many first time investors venture into house flipping without doing proper research and having a good understanding of what is involved. There are certain mistakes you should avoid falling into if you are a beginner at property flipping.

The Do's And Don'ts of Flipping Houses

To avoid making the same mistakes investors like you made at their early stage of property flipping, it would be best to find out what they are and avoid them.

Do's

Understand Everything Involved Before Buying a House

This is one of the essential rules when buying a property. Do your findings in advance to avoid unforeseen events. It would also save you from procuring unnecessary expenses. Evaluate the cost of the process involved before proceeding with your plans, if the cost would prevent you from making any substantial profit after selling then there is absolutely no point in buying the property.

Get an ARV Estimate from a More Reputable Source

Rather than relying on the ARV "after repair value" you find online, reach out to professionals in that field for a more reliable estimate. Local realtors in your surrounding can estimate just how much a particular property can be sold for in the neighborhood.

Build a Team

Although it might seem counterintuitive to hire a group of people to help out with the process involved in property flipping, it would save you money and time in the long run. Having a team work on a property will take less time and money and would enable you to sell off your property quicker and at a higher rate. Aside from a team of contractors, get a good real estate agent as their services cannot be overlooked.

Stick To Your Budget

Before you begin with your renovation plans, it is advisable to draw up a budget to avoid overspending and any form of confusion. To be on a safer side, ask any of the local contractors around you for a budget quote before purchasing the property. Ensure your contractor works following the budget and sticks to the plan.

Don'ts

Don't Go In Blind

A lot of people believe property flipping is something that could be learned during the process, but this is not always so. They also believe they can pick up the skill of house rehab when they find themselves in the position to do so.

Although a few things can be learned in the process, the longer the time it takes you to get things fixed the more money it would cost. With each passing day, your property stays in your possession and the more money you lose to various house maintenance bills.

Don't Just Use the ARV Online

When it comes to house flipping, investors are advised not to spend above 70% of the ARV when purchasing a house. You might be familiar with this principle, but it will be a complete waste to you if your ARV estimate is wrong.

Although it is nice to know the ARV of houses sold in your neighborhood, it is unwise to rely solely on the information gotten online. Several factors can contribute to the value of your property; therefore, you shouldn't depend on what you see online.

Don't Take On The Whole Project Yourself

TV reality shows are sometimes misleading. Sometimes it takes more than two people to run a project from start to finish, which is against what is portrayed on most flipping reality shows. There might be several areas in your property that require fixing. This would entail hiring expert hands to get them done.

Don't Spend Too Much Money

Renovation aims to improve the standard of the property to impress the buyer but do not procure expenses that would render you profitless.

Don't Be Cheap

Working on a limited budget shouldn't stop you from getting quality materials. Do not go for very low-quality materials all in the bid to cut down on expenses. The chances are you might find it a lot more difficult to sell out the property as the quality of the house materials would discourage potential buyers especially when it's meant to be a high-quality home.

Chapter 13: Final Checklist

There is a lot of work involved in flipping a house. Engaging in a full house remodel is essential. However, there is more. It is vital that you have a business plan, have a budget, and pull through some closing processes.

You have to do this without losing your patience or funds. With this, you soon realize that there is a lot of work done before construction.

Now that you intend to flip a house, what is next?

In the absence of adequate guidance, getting your first flip done might be a little tricky. Due to this, we have taken time to put down guidelines that can help you get this done quickly.

The House Flipping Checklist

To flip a house successfully, follow the following steps;

Come up with a Budget

Before starting a project, come up with a budget. You can include business loans, as well as your own money when coming up with a budget. With an idea of how much you are ready to spend, it would be less complicated for you to choose the kind of market to buy the essentials.

Always have it in mind that the lesser the amount you are willing to spend when setting out, the more the distance between you and popular cities. Your home might not also be able to compare with the most attractive homes in your environment as well. But it is not an issue. It will allow you to focus on renovations rather than spending your money making the actual purchase.

It is important to note that flipping a house in a low-income neighborhood means you will most likely sell the house to an investor that will go on to rent out the house. Doing this means you might make less money. Nevertheless, you will have a smoother sales process.

When starting to make flips, you should have a straightforward business plan. Also, do not deal in homes with some serious structural issue as these issues might make you lose a lot of money.

Obtain Financing

Getting your finances together is the next thing you should do after having a budget. You have to get the money together even before you need it. Do this by talking to investors as soon as you come up with a budget. With this, you can always get ready before its time for renovation. There are equally various loans you can take advantage of for flipping houses as we have discussed in earlier chapters.

Put Together a Reliable Team

Flipping a house is not a job for one person. You will need a team to do this the right way. This means you should make arrangements with local contractors while you search for houses to flip. Before going ahead to work with anyone, make sure there is a contract ready to be signed by both parties.

Locate a House you Will Like to Flip

It is evident that a lot of work goes into planning before the actual house flipping begins. So, if you are better prepared, the process will be a lot easier.

When looking for houses to flip, ensure that you purchase a house that is less than the market value. This is important because whatever profit you make will cover contractor fees, Realtor fees, the cost of renovation, and closing costs.

Put Up an Offer and Get the House Closed

When the time to purchase the house finally comes, there will be some level of competition. A lot of times, this competition will be against more experienced investors.

To beat more experienced investors to this, you will need the services of a home inspector. Once you have this, go on and make your offers.

Renovation Begins

Now is the time for renovations to begin. The quality of renovation and the duration of renovation are two critical things you have to take seriously. The reason for this is as soon as you close the property, you have to start paying utility bills and taxes.

Below are some things that will be involved in renovation;

General Exterior
- Fencing

- Driveway
- Landscaping
- HVAC System
- Roof
- Siding
- Septic System
- Patio/Deck
- General Interior
- Flooring
- Drywall Installation
- Paint
- Furniture staging
- Baseboards, moulding, and trim
- Plumbing
- Electric box wiring and protection

Bathroom
- Tub and Shower
- Flooring
- Counters
- Plumbing
- Toilet

- Tiling

Kitchen
- Electricity
- Counters
- Appliances
- Backsplash
- Plumbing

Sell It

At this point, the home is way better than it was when you purchased it. Now that it has an attractive appearance, you should sell it and make back all the money you put into renovating it alongside some good profit.

You can get the home sold easily by working with a Realtor. If you have issues with paying huge commissions, you can decide to work with a flat fee agent.

Flat fee agents are very affordable. As a result of this, there is no need to get a realtor license until you are more settled in business.

Chapter 14: Conclusion

The business of flipping houses can be one that comes with a lot of potential. However, you need to remember that it comes with its set of risks. Remember to not to go into flipping blindly, as doing so can result in a considerable amount of losses for you.

I have provided you with the necessary information you require. All you need to do is read, digest and effectively implement them, so the entire process is easy for you. What is left, is for you to come up with a strategy that works for you, which will ensure you make as much revenue as possible.

So why wait? Take the step now.

Bibliography

Flipping Houses for Profit - Tips for How to Flip a House. (2019). Retrieved from https://www.moneycrashers.com/five-tips-for-effectively-flipping-a-house/

5 Mistakes That Can Make House Flipping a Flop. (2019). Retrieved from https://www.investopedia.com/articles/mortgages-real-estate/08/house-flip.asp

Flipping. (2019). Retrieved from https://en.wikipedia.org/wiki/Flipping

How to Flip a House. (2019). Retrieved from https://www.daveramsey.com/blog/how-to-flip-a-house

Wood, M. (2019). How to Start a House-Flipping Business: Your Essential Toolkit - Fundera Ledger. Retrieved from https://www.fundera.com/blog/how-to-start-a-house-flipping-business

Garden, H., Garden, H., Estate, R., & Home, S. (2019). How House Flipping Works. Retrieved from https://home.howstuffworks.com/real-estate/selling-home/house-flipping.htm

How to flip a house: A step-by-step guide | LendingHome Blog. (2018). Retrieved from https://www.lendinghome.com/blog/how-to-flip-a-house-in-8-steps/

Flipping Houses 101 | Rehab Financial Group. Retrieved from https://rehabfinancial.com/flipping-houses-101

The Pros and Cons of Flipping a Property. (2019). Retrieved from https://www.thebalancesmb.com/pros-and-cons-of-flipping-a-property-2124830

White, S., White, S., & White, S. Why I'll Never Fix and Flip Houses Again. Retrieved from https://www.biggerpockets.com/blog/dont-flip-houses

How To Start Flipping Houses Like A Pro | FortuneBuilders. Retrieved from https://www.fortunebuilders.com/flipping-houses/

Ready to Start Flipping Houses? Here's How to Borrow Money. (2018). Retrieved from https://www.thebalance.com/loans-for-flipping-houses-4129189

Considering a career flipping houses? Read this first | this. Retrieved from https://this.deakin.edu.au/career/considering-a-career-flipping-houses-read-this-first

The 9-to-5 workday isn't just hated—it's obsolete. (2018). Retrieved from https://qz.com/work/1189605/the-9-to-5-workday-isnt-just-hated-its-obsolete/

Images, J. (2018). Do people even work 9-to-5 anymore?. Retrieved from https://www.marketplace.org/2018/05/28/business/ive-always-wondered/why-do-keep-using-9-5

7 Ways to Level Up your Mindset. (2018). Retrieved from https://medium.com/swlh/7-ways-to-level-up-your-mindset-5395fd103310

Baller, E. 10 Ways to Cultivate a Positive Mindset and Change Your Life. Retrieved from https://tinybuddha.com/blog/10-ways-cultivate-positive-mindset-change-life/

Alton, L. (2016). 7 Ways to Make Positive Thinking a Habit. Retrieved from https://www.success.com/7-practical-tips-to-achieve-a-positive-mindset/

LaCava, M. All The Math You Need to Succeed as a House Flipper. Retrieved from https://www.biggerpockets.com/blog/2012/11/03/flip-houses-formula-math/

The Flip Formula. Retrieved from http://www.123flip.com/education/the-flip-formula/

Why After Repair Value is Key in Real Estate Investing. (2018). Retrieved from https://www.thebalancesmb.com/arv-after-repair-value-in-real-estate-investing-2867053

DealMachine for Real Estate Investing. Retrieved from https://dealmachine.com/blog/beginners-guide-for-flipping

www.ingramcontent.com/pod-product-compliance
Lightning Source LLC
Chambersburg PA
CBHW021820170526
45157CB00007B/2661